01 14

A GUIDE TO THE *THIRTY-SEVEN*
PRACTICES OF A BODHISATTVA

A Guide to the *Thirty-Seven Practices of a Bodhisattva*

Dzatrul Ngawang Tenzin Norbu

FOREWORD BY

Dzogchen Ponlop Rinpoche

TRANSLATED BY

Christopher Stagg

SNOW LION

Snow Lion
An imprint of Shambhala Publications, Inc.
4720 Walnut Street
Boulder, Colorado 80301
www.shambhala.com

9 8 7 6 5 4 3 2 1

First Edition
Printed in the United States of America

⊛ This edition is printed on acid-free paper that meets the
American National Standards Institute z39.48 Standard.
♻ Shambhala Publications makes every attempt to print on recycled paper.
For more information please visit www.shambhala.com.

Snow Lion is distributed worldwide by Penguin Random House, Inc.,
and its subsidiaries.

LIBRARY OF CONGRESS CATALOGING-IN-PUBLICATION DATA
Names: Ṅag-dbaṅ-bstan-'dzin-nor-bu, Rdza Roṅ-phu Bla-ma, 1867–1940. |
Stagg, Christopher, translator. | Dzogchen Ponlop, Rinpoche, 1965–, writer of foreword.
Title: A guide to the thirty-seven practices of a bodhisattva / Ngawang Tenzin Norbu;
translated by Christopher Stagg; foreword by Dzogchen Ponlop Rinpoche.
Other titles: Rgyal sras lag len so bdun gyi 'grel pa gźuṅ daṅ gdams ṅag zuṅ 'jug Bdud
rtsi'i bum bzaṅ. English
Description: First edition. | Boulder: Snow Lion, 2020. | Translation of: Rgyal sras lag
len so bdun gyi 'grel pa gźuṅ daṅ gdams ṅag zuṅ 'jug Bdud rtsi'i bum bzaṅ. | Includes
bibliographical references and index.
Identifiers: LCCN 2019037331 | ISBN 9781559394918 (hardback)
Subjects: LCSH: Rgyal-sras Thogs-med Bzang-po-dpal, 1295–1369. Rgyal-sras lag len so
bdun ma—Commentaries. | Enlightenment (Buddhism)—Requisites. | Religious life—
Bka'-gdams-pa (Sect)
Classification: LCC BQ4399.N3313 2020 | DDC 294.3/442—dc23
LC record available at https://lccn.loc.gov/2019037331

Contents

Foreword

In our day-to-day life situations, we are presented with all kinds of challenges. When we look outside, we find dire situations everywhere in the world affecting people, animals, and our environment. And when we look inside, we find the ups and downs of our physical, mental, and emotional experiences that fluctuate as unpredictably as the stock market. In the midst of all the chaos, it seems difficult to find a peaceful spot or kindness for each other in our lives.

The Thirty-Seven Practices of a Bodhisattva presents an alternative way of thinking, of relating to the outer and inner worlds of everyday living. It is a refreshing, revolutionary, and radical approach to a life that is worth exploring.

This Book

In the traditional framework of Mahayana wisdom, the revolutionary approach presented in this book is known as the bodhisattva way, the heroic path of the mind of wakefulness. Thus, *The Thirty-Seven Practices* is a training manual for thinking outside of our usual boxes of culture, religion, and self-centeredness. If your approach of thinking *inside* the box has worked well and fulfilled your dreams of happiness, *The Thirty-Seven Practices* is not a must-have manual. The root text contains thirty-seven key points for working with our mind, first through taming—finding a way to bring the mind home, to a state of calmness and clarity—and then through cultivating the heart of kindness and compassion. It is, in fact, a practical guide on how to follow the path of the bodhisattvas, verse by verse.

By way of a brief literary background, this practical manual of working with *bodhichitta*, the awakening heart, belongs to the Mahayana's Kadampa school, founded by the Indian master Atisha (982–1054). The connotation of Kadampa is that all the words (*ka*) of the Buddha are taken as personal instructions (*dampa*). Thus there are no words left behind in books as mere theory; they are all applied in action as practice. The Kadampas emphasize the gradual, stage-by-stage path known as the *lamrim* ("stages of the path") approach of the three types of individuals; one of their main contemplative methods is the use of guiding maxims or verses, such as the slogans of *lojong* ("training the mind" or "mind transformation").

The three renowned and indispensable guidebooks of the Indian and Tibetan Mahayana tradition are Langthangpa's (1054–1123) *Eight Verses of Training the Mind,* which is the shortest, most condensed work; Tokmé's *Thirty-Seven Practices,* the medium-length text;* and Shantideva's (685–763) *Bodhicharyavatara,* or *Entrance to the Way of a Bodhisattva,* the extensive presentation.

THE AUTHOR OF THE ROOT TEXT

The Thirty-Seven Practices was written by Dharmabhadra Ngulchu Tokmé (685–763). He was born in a small town in the Tsang region of Tibet. From birth, he showed great qualities of kindness and compassion; for example, in his early childhood, in the midst of a bitterly cold winter, he saw a heap of small insects freezing to death. Unable to bear the sight, he took off his only garment and covered them with it. Tokmé's childhood was not an easy one. He lost his mother and father at the tender ages of three and five, respectively, and was thereafter raised by his maternal uncle. Despite this intense hardship, he seized his misfortune as an opportunity to discover and follow the path of the Buddha's Mahayana teachings.

Tokmé studied with many great masters of his time, including Butön (1290–1364), and it was during his early years of study that he received the name of Tokmé ("unhindered," referring to his capacity for understanding and learning). He later studied and mastered the Five Treatises of Maitreya/Asanga, which strongly influenced his view and practice of the Mahayana path.

Ngulchu is the name of the region in central-western Tibet where Tokmé lived and wrote his famed text. Since then, *The Thirty-Seven Practices* has gained the status of one of the foremost Tibetan-authored sourcebooks for kindness and compassion, the journey of the Mahayana lifestyle.

---

*Alternatively, Chekhawa's (1101–1175) renowned *Seven Points of Mind Training* may be regarded as the medium-length member of the trilogy.

THE AUTHOR OF THE COMMENTARY

The Thirty-Seven Practices is further elucidated in *A Guide to the Thirty-Seven Practices of a Bodhisattva* by the nineteenth-century Tibetan master Dzatrul Ngawang Tenzin Norbu (1867–1940; see Translator's Introduction). The commentary explains not just the root text's theory but also its experiential meaning and how to put each of these verses directly into practice. In this way, Dzatrul's work is indispensable, exceptional, and noteworthy. Even those who are already familiar with the root text will surely see its verses in a new light through Dzatrul's instructions.

THE TRANSLATOR

Christopher Stagg was my dear friend and student, an accomplished music teacher, and a practitioner-translator. Chris studied the Tibetan language, Buddhist philosophy, and meditation for decades and became known for his skill in teaching, translation work, and musical composition. Chris not only taught but treasured and lived these principles, and he expressed them in action, through being genuinely kind, compassionate, and tolerant to all. I had the opportunity to work with him on his translation of this book as well as his translation of Milarepa's *Hundred Thousand Songs*, the classic collection of *dohas* from the yogic tradition of Vajrayana Buddhism. Chris's translations are gentle, rich, easy to understand, and accessible, just like his character.

My heartfelt gratitude and appreciation goes to all the authors and especially to the translator, Christopher Stagg, for making this classic wisdom of the world available for English readers.

Chris's untimely passing is a great loss for all of us, and I truly miss his humor, friendship, and wisdom. Nevertheless, this gift of Chris's—the wealth of wisdom and compassion—brings a smile in the heart for all those who seek relief from this world's self-centeredness and suffering.

I would like to thank Rita Stagg, Chris's mother, for her permission to publish this book and for her kindness and loving spirit, which unmistakably echoes throughout Chris's words of wisdom and compassion here.

May this world discover the light of innate wisdom, embedded within every mind, and manifest love and kindness, the nature of all hearts.

Dzogchen Ponlop Rinpoche
Nalanda West, Seattle, WA
May 2019

Editors' Preface

Christopher Stagg, the translator, annotator, and introducer of the present volume, had, by September 2018, completed all of the translations of this book and had begun communicating with Shambhala Publications about the process of finalizing the manuscript. He had chosen and received the publisher's approval for the book's title and had begun the final round of editing on his introduction, translations, and endnotes. Yet on October 1, 2018, just weeks after his forty-first birthday, Chris passed away tragically in an automobile accident in Seattle, Washington, U.S.A. A loving family and spiritual community, as well as countless others who were touched by his life, continue to grieve. Although his untimely departure is an unspeakable loss, a healthy portion of his legacy will live on in his translations and written works. We are delighted to present just one set of these works here.

A team of volunteer editors from Chris's sangha, Nalandabodhi, helped put the finishing touches on the manuscript in consultation with Shambhala Publications. In particular, Cindy Shelton, Leon Marcus, and Tyler Dewar did further editing for uniformity of style; Tyler Dewar made modifications to the text in multiple locations where there seemed to be minor lingering translation issues. As a group, we took an approach of allowing the clarity of Chris's writing and translation to speak for itself. Some endnotes were added when further context seemed to be called for. Additional specific editorial decisions are explained in the notes to the sections where those edits occurred. We have also added a brief word about Chris's life and activities at the end of this book; we hope this will enhance readers' appreciation of the context and remarkable dharma practice from which this book was born. We would like to express our sincere appreciation for the fabulous work of Casey Kemp, who guided the entire publication process, and of Tracy Davis, who copyedited the book and made many key suggestions to improve the text.

We rejoice in Chris's example of seizing the preciousness of the impermanent and finite human life span to accomplish genuine good for self and other. The powerful elucidation and celebration of the bodhisattva path contained in this book seem to us a most fitting punctuation mark for our esteemed friend, colleague, and teacher's bodhisattva journey to full awakening.

Translator's Acknowledgments

I am deeply indebted to Dzogchen Ponlop Rinpoche, who encouraged me to take on this project, and who has been an untiring guide for all of his students. He is a living example of the teachings put forth in this text, and his activity to benefit others is truly astounding in both scope and effectiveness.

I would also like to thank Acharya Tashi Wangchuk and Mitra Karl Brunnhölzl, who, with their many years of experience in studying Tibetan texts, have both very generously spent numerous hours with me to help clarify and render into English the more difficult points of the original. Karl's voice is also strongly present in the translation of the opening homage and the concluding verses of the commentary. Thank you also to Mitra Tyler Dewar for his availability for a few brief but very helpful consultations on terminology and language resources. A special thank-you goes to Khenpo Sherap Phuntsok of Thrangu Monastery, who helped in clarifying some questions in the final stages.

In translating the root text, I referenced previous translations by Michele Martin, the Padmakara Translation Group, and Ruth Sonam. These translations were of some assistance in cultivating a broader sense of how to render the Tibetan into English in a new and meaningful way.

Kimberly Colwell helped in editing the English and was instrumental in clearing up many of the "Tibetanisms" in the first draft of the translation, as well as providing a copyedit, thus making the final version much more readable. Thanks also go to Richard Carkeek of the University of Washington East Asia Library, who provided reference help.

Stephanie Johnston, tireless leader of Nalandabodhi Publications, contributed generously to the process of bringing the production of the book to completion.

And finally, my heartfelt thanks go to Sherab Tenzin of Rumtek Monastery, who initially input the Tibetan text into an easily readable format during my first stay in Nepal and was a tremendous help to me in the initial stages of the translation.

All mistakes contained herein are completely my own, and I pray that they be forgiven. I genuinely aspire that this book be of benefit to all who may come across it. May it be the cause for many beings to progress along the path of awakening, and may they, in turn, be of great benefit to limitless others.

Christopher Stagg
Sarnath, UP, India
February 2013

———

Seattle, WA
September 2018

TRANSLATOR'S INTRODUCTION

Gyalse Ngulchu Tokmé Zangpo's text *The Thirty-Seven Practices of a Bodhisattva* has become well known among Western Buddhists and is frequently taught and referenced by contemporary teachers in the Tibetan tradition. There are now at least ten English translations available, many published with commentaries by great modern-day masters such as His Holiness the Fourteenth Dalai Lama, His Holiness the Seventeenth Gyalwang Karmapa, and His Holiness Dilgo Khyentse Rinpoche.

New translations of a text can provide new perspectives for those who wish to get closer to the meaning and feel of the original but are unable to read the source language. Readers also naturally connect more with the voice of one translator than another, merely based on inclination and preference, so a variety of translations to choose from can be helpful. Since the perfect translation doesn't exist, this newly rendered English version of *The Thirty-Seven Practices of a Bodhisattva* may thus bear some merit, and other translations may hit the mark more aptly in other ways. While it is my hope that another translation of the root text will be of benefit, the primary highlight of this publication is the commentary elucidation of the root text by the twentieth-century Nyingma master Dzatrul Ngawang Tenzin Norbu[1] (1867–1940), translated here into English for the first time.

Dzatrul Ngawang Tenzin Norbu's exposition of *The Thirty-Seven Practices of a Bodhisattva* is one of the most extensive traditionally written commentaries on *The Thirty-Seven Practices of a Bodhisattva* available in Tibet. Relied on and referenced often, particularly by the Nyingma tradition, the original Tibetan has been republished in modern book format by the Library of Tibetan Works and Archives (LTWA).[2] Additionally included in this publication, also for the first time in English, is a short *sadhana* practice composed by the commentator with the aim of aiding interested students in deepening their understanding and experience of the practices taught here. The sadhana, titled *The Swift Path to Awakening*, is a meditation on Avalokiteshvara in the form of a guru yoga and deity yoga, as well as a contemplation on each of the root verses. The sadhana is the focus of part three of this volume.

THE AUTHOR OF *THE THIRTY-SEVEN PRACTICES OF A BODHISATTVA*, GYALSE NGULCHU TOKMÉ ZANGPO

Gyalse Ngulchu Tokmé Zangpo (ca. 1295–ca. 1369), or, in short form, Ngulchu Tokmé, was born in Tsang, the central region of Tibet, near Sakya Monastery. Stories of his life describe how even as a young boy he displayed an exceptional outpouring of compassion and deep concern for friends, animals, and even seemingly insentient objects. Such consideration for others and disregard for his own personal interests throughout his life earned him the name Gyalse, or "Son of the Victors," a Tibetan epithet for a bodhisattva.[3]

Renowned during his lifetime as a great scholar, he extensively studied the various traditions of Buddhism within Tibet, from sutra to tantra. At the age of only fifteen, he so eruditely clarified a difficult point of Asanga's text the *Abhidharmasamuccaya* that his colleagues and teachers gave him the name Tokmé, the Tibetans' name for Asanga.[4] Ngulchu Tokmé thus broadly demonstrated the two qualities of great compassion and superior knowledge (wisdom), the bases for all Mahayana Buddhist practice.

The Thirty-Seven Practices of a Bodhisattva is a brief text included within both the lojong and lamrim genres of Tibetan Buddhist literature. These two genres were first propagated by the Kadampa lineage of Atisha and his disciples, and later codified by Tsongkhapa, the founder of today's Geluk school of Tibetan Buddhism, with particular focus on the lamrim. Scholars consider Ngulchu Tokmé, whose life span overlapped Tsongkhapa's, to be a later commentator of these literary traditions (see the lineage chart of the Kadampa teachings in appendix 2).

LAMRIM (STAGES OF THE PATH)

The Thirty-Seven Practices follows the format of the lamrim, or the stages of the path teachings. Considered to have been first taught in Atisha's *Bodhipathapradipa* (*Lamp for the Path of Awakening*), this format categorizes all of the practices of the Buddhist path into those of lesser, middling, and great beings, in successive order. The lamrim teachings help practitioners develop stability in their understanding by presenting the practices in a progressive way, later practices requiring deep familiarity with those that come before. Ngulchu Tokmé presents the thirty-seven practices in the lamrim format and declaims at the end of each verse that each is "the practice of a bodhisattva"—someone who aims to help all sentient beings attain full spiritual awakening.

Verses 1 through 7 present the preliminary practices for the lamrim. These contemplations help the practitioner orient their mind away from worldly concerns and focus on spiritual matters. The preliminaries culminate in the taking of refuge, or making a full commitment to following the Buddhist path.

Verse 8 embarks on the lamrim proper with the practice of "lesser beings." The primary focus of this stage is the abandonment of unwholesome actions, which were taught by the Buddha to be the direct cause of suffering. This practice includes the contemplation of the various so-called lower realms of sentient beings, with a horrific depiction of the sufferings that must be endured by those who have engaged in a great number of unwholesome deeds. The three lower realms include the various hell realms, the hungry-ghost (*preta*) realms, and the animal realm. Westerners, particularly in our scientifically oriented, postmodern culture, often have difficulty subscribing to the literal descriptions in these teachings. Past and future lives, other realms of existence, ghosts, and the like are not generally part of our socially accepted view of the universe. However, even if we do not accept this view at first, looking closely at our own lives, it is not difficult to see that after acting under the influence of negative emotions we experience suffering in an immediate way. Likewise, if we perform positive actions, we experience happiness. Modern Western audiences do not always connect well with scare tactics; however, one cannot deny the efficacy of fear as a motivator, and this is the approach of the practices taught for the benefit of lesser beings.

Next, verse 9 describes the practice of middling beings. Here, the focus is on the ephemeral nature of happiness within cyclic existence (*samsara*). While the pleasure we experience may seem, at first, to be positive, this practice encourages the practitioner to recognize that such pleasures are merely passing and that attachment to them only intensifies one's suffering. It shows that even if one accumulates enough positive actions to obtain a comfortable situation, such a situation is only temporary, "like dewdrops on a blade of grass." Thus, inspired by reflection on this teaching, one develops revulsion for such transitory, worldly happiness and strives only to attain the ultimate happiness of liberation.

Finally, verse 10 begins the presentation of the practice of great beings, the primary focus of the Mahayana path as well as the remainder of Ngulchu Tokmé's text. This is divided into two categories: the practice of relative bodhichitta, namely exchanging self for other; and absolute bodhichitta, or developing an understanding and experience of nonreferential wisdom. While the teachings on relative bodhichitta provide suggestions on how to work with various situations in daily life to reduce self-clinging, the approach of absolute bodhichitta is to experience directly all phenomena, including one's "self," as being without essence or, to use the language of the Mahayana, as being of the nature of emptiness. It is taught that if one has a direct experience and realization of emptiness, one will spontaneously manifest all other bodhisattva qualities such as loving-kindness and compassion.

Following the discussion of relative and absolute bodhichitta, most lamrim presentations include a brief introduction to tantric, or Vajrayana, practice. Such practices, while they provide skillful methods to help further the direct experience of emptiness, do not teach any higher view than what is already presented in the teachings of absolute bodhichitta of the general Mahayana. While there is no mention of tantra in Ngulchu Tokmé's text, the commentator Ngawang Tenzin Norbu occasionally relies on quotations from the tantras to show that, although it does not explicitly include any such tantric descriptions, *The Thirty-Seven Practices* contains complete instructions for the path to full awakening.

Lojong (Mind Training)

While the lamrim teachings provide a bird's-eye view of practice on the Mahayana Buddhist path, the lojong genre of teachings concentrates specifically on the cultivation of relative and absolute bodhichitta and on working practically and directly with one's personal situation in everyday life. Works from this genre typically offer a pithy set of verses or slogans for monastics as well as laypeople who may not have time to study the vast quantity of Buddhist sutras and treatises. Ngulchu Tokmé remained true to this tradition with *The Thirty-Seven Practices of a Bodhisattva*, which contains an explanation of the entire Mahayana path in a mere forty-three verses: two opening stanzas, one verse for each of the thirty-seven practices themselves, and four concluding verses. Because of its brevity and direct applicability, this text is often one of the first that young Tibetan monastic students memorize in their education.

THE AUTHOR OF THE COMMENTARY, DZATRUL NGAWANG TENZIN NORBU

Dzatrul Rinpoche, Ngawang Tenzin Norbu (1867–1940), the author of this commentary on *The Thirty-Seven Practices of a Bodhisattva*, founded the Nyingmapa Rongpu Monastery situated on the northern slopes of Mount Everest in southern Tibet, as well as other monasteries in the Solokhumbu region of Nepal. Born in Upper Kharta in the Phakdru district of southern Tibet, in his youth Dzatrul Rinpoche engaged in monastic studies at Mindroling Monastery and completed a three-year retreat, although by that time he was no stranger to retreat practice, having already endured many hardships practicing in Padmasambhava's cave at Rongpu. While at Mindroling, he met his primary teacher, the great tertön[5] Trulshik Kunzang Thongdrol (1862–1922), who asked him to build a monastery in Rongpu. There, in 1901, Dzatrul Rinpoche established Do-ngak Zungjuk Chöling[6] ("Place of the Union of Sutra and Tantra"), where he established his seat, emphasized strict discipline, and guided many ascetic monastics, both monks and nuns, in solitary retreat.[7] Prior to Ngawang Tenzin Norbu's tenure, a tradition of noncelibate temples had developed in the Khumbu region, and it was due in large part to Dzatrul's influence that celibate monasteries were established and began to flourish there.[8]

While not widely known throughout Tibetan culture, Dzatrul, locally known as "the buddha of Rongpu," was highly influential and respected in the region and was the foremost lama for the Khumbu Sherpas. Indeed, it was Ngawang Tenzin Norbu who gave Tenzing Norgay, the Sherpa famed for summiting Mount Everest with Sir Edmund Hillary in 1953, the name he is known by.[9] As Rongpu Monastery is located near the Everest north base camp, it was common for many climbers to encounter Dzatrul on the way to their ascent.[10] A British climber, C. G. Bruce, described his encounter with the Rinpoche in 1922:

> This particular Lama was beyond question a remarkable individual. He was a large, well-made man of about 60, full of dignity, with a most intelligent and wise face and an extraordinarily attractive smile.[11]

In addition to his portrayal as a charismatic and accomplished spiritual master, Dzatrul was a capable, effective leader and administrator. Though he spent much of his life in retreat at Rongpu, his activity was vast: he founded monasteries and festivals and performed important rituals for Buddhist followers in the region. It was because of Dzatrul's influence that the renowned Tengboche Monastery was founded near the Nepali base camp of Mount Everest.[12] Dzatrul also had strong ties with and significant financial support from the nearby Tibetan town of Dingri. One observer wrote:

> Since its establishment, Dza-rong [Rongpu Monastery] has been an independent monastery enjoying autonomy from outside authority. The growth of its power and influence was the outcome of hard work and good leadership—the efforts of Ngawang-ten-dzin. It was he who secured the patronage of wealthy D'ing-ri agricuturalists [sic] and traders. . . . By the time of his death in 1940 the Dza-rong Lama enjoyed the patronage of virtually all [of] D'ing-ri's rural population, as well as that of leading Sherpa families in the adjacent regions.[13]

Dzatrul Rinpoche's foremost student was Trulshik Rinpoche, Ngawang Chökyi Lodrö (1923–2011), who succeeded him as abbot at the age of only nineteen upon Dzatrul's death. During the Chinese Cultural Revolution in 1959, Trulshik Rinpoche fled to Nepal, where he founded his present seat, Thubten Chöling.

THE EXCELLENT VASE OF NECTAR, A COMMENTARY ON *THE THIRTY-SEVEN PRACTICES OF A BODHISATTVA*

Though many of the original woodblocks of Ngawang Tenzin Norbu's writings were destroyed during the Cultural Revolution, in recent years his works have been reassembled from sources both in and outside of Tibet and have been published as a set of nine large volumes. This commentary, *The Excellent Vase of Nectar: The Union of Scripture and Oral Instructions, a Commentary on "The Thirty-Seven Practices of a Bodhisattva,"* is his best-known work.

As do many Tibetans, it seems that Dzatrul felt the importance and usefulness of the text for beginning practitioners, as he listed it first among topics of study for monks and nuns in the codes of discipline[14] he composed for Tengboche and Drakmar Chöling, two of the branch monasteries of Rongpu.[15]

In his autobiography, Dzatrul Rinpoche mentions that during *yarne* (the traditional monastic summer retreat) at Rongpu in 1903, he gave a twenty-day teaching consisting of two sessions each day on *The Thirty-Seven Practices of a Bodhisattva*, with just over sixty students present. In addition to the main teaching sessions, he also had them engage in additional review sessions, and at the conclusion of the teaching he conferred bodhisattva vows on all present. Subsequently, the students requested that he compose a commentary on the text. Dzatrul writes:

> Because those who were assembled had taken inadequate notes,[16] and emphatically requested that a guidance text be composed, using the previous textual outline of the Bodhisattva [Ngulchu Tokmé] and a word commentary by Dome Khen Sönam Rinpoche as a basis, I began writing *The Excellent Vase of Nectar: The Union of Scripture and Oral Instructions*.[17]

The colophon of the commentary mentions that the request was made again and again in particular by "the supreme rare omniscient one of the residence in Phakdru," who appears to be the retired khenpo, Könchok Drukdrak, though it seems unlikely that he was one of those present who took "inadequate notes."[18] Dzatrul recounts that at the end of the fall of the following year, while on personal retreat, "Apart from occasionally working on writing the extensive commentary on *The Thirty-Seven Practices of a Bodhisattva* during the session breaks, I had little other distraction."[19] Though his autobiography makes no further mention of the commentary, according to the colophon of the text it was completed during the next year, that of the Wood Snake (1905), at his residence at Rongpu Monastery, when Dzatrul was forty years old.

Dome Khen Sönam Rinpoche, mentioned above in the quotation from Dzatrul's autobiography as the author of one of the texts he referred to while writing his own, is almost certainly Minyak Kunzang Sönam (1823–1905), the great Gelukpa scholar and direct disciple of Dza Patrul Rinpoche. Using his monastic name, Thubten Chökyi Drakpa, he too composed a commentary of the same name, *The Excellent Vase of Nectar: The Union of Scripture and Oral Instructions*,[20] predating Dzatrul's. The subtitle of both of these authors' texts, *The Union of Scripture and Oral Instructions,* is in harmony with the approach of the Kadampa lineage masters who regarded any statement by the Buddha, whether it is of a philosophical or a technical nature, as a practical instruction to be brought into one's direct experience, just as a spiritual teacher would orally instruct their students.

In Chökyi Drakpa's work, the commentary for each verse follows a consistent format. After the root verse is stated, Chökyi Drakpa gives (1) a word commentary; (2) supporting quotations from sutras and treatises from India; (3) statements from Kadampa masters; and (4) quotations from Ngulchu Tokmé himself. The format of Dzatrul's commentary is clearly inspired by this, drawing from many of the same sources, but it draws additionally from further sutras, even tantras, and from a variety of different Tibetan masters, making his own commentary more extensive. Like Chökyi Drakpa, Dzatrul also frequently gives additional commentary of his own in connection with the supporting quotations.

The longest commentary on a single verse is for verse 29, which discusses the *paramita* of meditative concentration. Here, Dzatrul Rinpoche gives an overview of the tradition of meditation as taught in the Buddhism of Tibet. This includes a summary of the various types of mundane and transcendent absorptions, as well as practical instruction on how to cultivate the practice of *shamatha*, or calm abiding.

In the commentary on verse 30, on the paramita of *prajna*, or wisdom, Dzatrul Rinpoche briefly discusses the traditional reasonings used to come to resolution about the view of emptiness. After presenting this dialectical approach, Dzatrul provides quotations and instructions that are in harmony with the more direct approaches of pointing out the nature of mind found in the traditions of Vajrayana, Mahamudra, and Dzogchen. Here, Dzatrul defines the meditation of prajna as remaining, "fresh, uncontrived, and perfectly free from all extremes of elaboration."

Dzatrul's commentary fills in all of the details of the framework of Ngulchu Tokme's text, providing the reader with an in-depth study of the complete Mahayana path.

THE SWIFT PATH TO AWAKENING, A COMPANION SADHANA PRACTICE

The third part of this book focuses on a practice for deepening and internalizing one's understanding of *The Thirty-Seven Practices* on a more intuitive level. Titled *The Swift Path to Awakening: A Supplementary Practice That*

Breaks "The Thirty-Seven Practices of a Bodhisattva" into Sessions,[21] the liturgy was written about ten years after Dzatrul completed the commentary. You might say that studying and contemplating the commentary takes a "left-brained" approach to *The Thirty-Seven Practices,* and doing this practice uses a "right-brained" approach: relying on intuition and employing imaginative visualization. It takes the traditional form of a type of devotional liturgy called *sadhana,* which literally means "method for accomplishment." Using the bodhisattva Avalokiteshvara, the embodiment of compassion, as a support and focus, the main practice here is to open one's heart and, in a sense, intuitively merge with the essence of compassion and awakening. Where Dzatrul's commentary on the root text employs reason and intellect for bringing about understanding of *The Thirty-Seven Practices of a Bodhisattva,* his meditation practice employs contemplation, intuition, and visualization to evoke genuine experience within the heart of the practitioner.

In this age of science and reason, when even spirituality can be framed in rational terms, the intuitive heart of spirituality often gets deemphasized. The inclusion of this sadhana practice serves as a counterpoint to the necessary, but also limited, approach of intellectual understanding and contemplation. Here, with our intellectual understanding as a basis, we train in letting go and leaping into a direct experience of embodying the practices by way of supplication. This approach is tied to the traditional practice of guru yoga.

At this point it seems important to make a few clarifying remarks about what the word *guru* means. In today's English vernacular, the word can take on an almost pejorative connotation, but in Sanskrit, it has the literal meaning of being heavy, or weighty with positive qualities. In its outer form, the guru refers to an individual who has positive qualities and is able to help instill those same qualities in others. However, there are different ways of thinking about guru, and in the end, the real guru is one's own inner guru, own's own awakened mind, which everyone possesses. Here, supplicating the guru takes the form of supplicating the outer guru, in the form of Avalokiteshvara, in order to awaken and make the inner guru fully manifest. So, in this practice, we mix our minds with Avalokiteshvara's ultimate compassionate mind, in essence inviting our own dormant awakened qualities to fully manifest. Of course, we cannot actually mix our own minds with anyone else's, but through this type of sadhana, we evoke something that is already present within us. How do we go about doing this? In this practice we start by simply engendering a sense of confidence, genuine interest, and respect toward Avalokiteshvara as the embodiment of compassion. Then we follow the instructions as they appear in the liturgy: supplicating, offering, paying homage, and so forth. With a heart of openness, we try as best we can to generate whatever is presented in the liturgy.

Sadhanas, which belong to a tradition going back to ancient India, are typically written in a set format. Likewise, this sadhana contains many elements that may be foreign to someone who is not familiar with this type of practice. Here I will briefly describe the meaning of each major section of the liturgy and how to practice it. However, it should be noted that nearly every element of the sadhana could be explicated for many pages, and in fact a number of texts from the Tibetan canon could be referenced to clarify a single element alone. While this description will be far from exhaustive, it should give the beginner at least a basic understanding of how to do the practice and to connect with it at the most essential level. For the enthusiast, that understanding can then be gradually expanded and supplemented through further study.

The sadhana opens with a short homage to Avalokiteshvara, the Great Compassionate One. Here it is important to understand that, while Avalokiteshvara is personified and described with specific physical features, he is more a principle than an actual individual. Of course, traditionally, he is seen as an individual, and this is a skillful method for those of us who are also individuals to connect with the principle that he embodies. But if we relate to Avalokiteshvara merely as an external, clearly defined (male!) entity who is solid and superior to ourselves, then we are missing out on the full scope of who and what Avalokiteshvara actually is. The external Avalokiteshvara, inseparable from the guru, is nothing but a symbolic representation of compassion on all its levels, which in turn is something all of us naturally already possess. But because we are not able to see that clearly at this stage of our path, we use imagery and symbolism as a provisional representation of this ultimate meaning.

Next, we recite a four-line verse on taking refuge. Dzatrul describes the meaning of refuge extensively in his commentary on verse 7 of *The Thirty-Seven Practices*. Here, we are saying that we cannot attain awakening completely on our own and that we must rely on the individuals and teachings that can help us the most effectively on this path. These are the Buddha, dharma, and sangha, which are explained in Dzatrul's commentary, as well as the guru, *yidam*, and *dakinis*, which could be described as internal, more subtle manifestations of the Buddha, dharma, and sangha. There are now many publications that describe these forms of refuge in detail, so I direct the reader to those for further explanation. Finally, we recite that we take refuge in our own mind. This is the real refuge: our own potential to be fully awakened and fully compassionate.

As with all Mahayana practices, next we focus on the generation of bodhichitta, the desire to attain awakening in order to benefit all sentient beings. Specifically, the lines state that we will practice guru yoga and deity yoga as a profound method to bring us to that state. There is a great deal that could be said about guru yoga and deity yoga, and it has been briefly described above. In essence, both practices, often performed inseparably (as they are here), consist of intuitively merging with the experience of awakening, accessible to all of us, by using these seemingly external representations as a provisional support.

The eighteen-line section of the liturgy that follows describes the visualization that we generate as a support for connecting with the principle of Avalokiteshvara. The liturgy itself provides the instruction on what to do; we simply visualize what is explained. These lines describe the form of Avalokiteshvara as well as his retinue. The most important point here is to have a sense that this great compassionate being, or energy, is actually present in front of us. Often, practitioners new to visualization feel intimidated and deficient, unable to visualize a clear image. One should take consolation in the fact that it is rare for someone to be able to visualize clearly right from the very beginning.

It is important to relax and have an attitude of playful creativity with visualizations. The traditional instruction for developing a clear visualization is to find a visual image of the main figure, a photograph or painting. (Avalokiteshvara, here depicted with four arms, is a common image that can be easily found online or at various Buddhist bookstores.) We then look at the image for some time in a relaxed way without thinking much about it, and once we feel some familiarity with the image, look away, and simply see if we can recall the image in our mind. If that recalled image becomes unclear, we look again at the picture. We alternate in this way between looking at the photo and recalling the image mentally until some sense of clarity develops. In the beginning, however, the sense of presence is more important than the visual details of the visualization. We should try to have a genuine sense that the embodiment of compassion is actually present right before us. We could half-jokingly refer to the practice as a "feelization." The visualization should incorporate all the senses; we should try to really feel that Avalokiteshvara is here with us. This is generally a pleasant and joyful practice, so we should not add the element of worrying about getting it right. We simply do our best with the descriptions and instructions that are provided and connect primarily with the love and compassion of Avalokiteshvara as a reflection of our own true nature.

After we have generated the "feelization," we then relate or interact with it. The next few verses end with the line, "I supplicate the glorious guru." At this stage we are connecting further with the principle of guru yoga as described above.

The following verses then go through the traditional seven-branch prayer, a way to accumulate merit and open one's heart further. The seven branches are prostrating, offering, confessing, rejoicing, requesting to teach, requesting to remain, and dedicating. This is followed by a mandala offering and a supplication to the lineage of *The Thirty-Seven Practices of a Bodhisattva*.

At this point, we visualize that light emanates from the syllable HRIH, which is in the heart center of Avalokiteshvara. This light strikes all of the retinue that surrounds him; they then melt into light and dissolve back into him. Then Avalokiteshvara moves from the space in front of us to the crown of our own head, and we recite a sixfold supplication three times. The preliminary section concludes with further visualization and supplication connected to a specific one of the thirty-seven practices.

Dzatrul formatted this sadhana so that each session is devoted to the contemplation of one of the thirty-seven practices. The sections dealing with the actual bodhisattva practices serve as a template with the text to be substituted for each session in bold type. The first of these—contemplating the freedoms and resources of this human life and engaging diligently in hearing, contemplating, and meditating on the dharma—is explicitly written out in the liturgy. For subsequent sessions, using the text as it appears in the sadhana as a template, one substitutes the words printed in bold type with the appropriate text for that practice, as presented in Dzatrul's explanation following the main sadhana liturgy.

After the preliminaries, the main practice focuses on the recitation and contemplation of actual verses from the root text. Each session is intended to take a single verse as a contemplation, as we read the verse verbatim except for a single change in the last line. Instead of ending with ". . . is the practice of a bodhisattva," here it is expressed as an aspiration and supplication: "May [this practice] arise in our mind streams." We contemplate the verse for however long we wish, and then conclude the main practice with yet another visualization and supplication to be able to come to embody the particular bodhisattva practice.

Finally, for the concluding practice, we change focus from Avalokiteshvara being supplicated externally to meditating on ourselves actually becoming the guru Avalokiteshvara. This section begins with supplicating Avalokiteshvara at the crown of our head. He then dissolves into us, and we actually become Avalokiteshvara. At this point, we recite the six-syllable mantra as much as possible. While doing the mantra recitation, we visualize light radiating out to all sentient beings, who themselves also become Avalokiteshvara.

After concluding our mantra recitation, we allow our mind to relax and for a brief time rest nonreferentially, without any thought. When thoughts arise again, we conclude with the verses of dedication and aspiration, thus completing the formal sadhana practice session.

For the postmeditation period—the "normal life" time after the formal meditation session—Dzatrul instructs that we should contemplate the thirty-seven practices further by looking at commentaries and scripture, and maintain mindfulness and awareness throughout our day.

At the very end, Dzatrul includes all of the different iterations of the bodhisattva practices to be used and inserted for the respective sessions, outlined in accord with the way they are each presented in his own commentary on the root text.

A Note on the Source Text

I obtained the primary edition of the commentary used for this translation from the Tibetan collection of the East Asia Library of the University of Washington in Seattle. The book, in traditional *pecha* format, was printed in 1970 from the Rongpu woodblocks now kept at Thubten Chöling Monastery in Nepal. I also compared this edition with the version published by the Library of Tibetan Works and Archives (LTWA) (2006) and the edition found in the Collected Works of Dzatrul Ngawang Tenzin Norbu (2004).[22] I also referenced the Collected Works version (2004) downloaded from the Buddhist Digital Resource Center (BDRC) in the final stages of editing. The 1970 Rongpu printing and the Collected Works version seem to be more complete than the LTWA edition, as large passages are missing from the latter, particularly under the commentaries for verses 29 and 30. All discrepancies I found have been noted in the text.

PART ONE

THE ROOT TEXT

*The Thirty-Seven Practices
of a Bodhisattva*

Although he sees that all phenomena are free of coming and going,
He strives only for the benefit of beings.
To the protector Avalokiteshvara and the supreme guru
I continually pay homage with my three gates. (A)

The sources of benefit and happiness, the perfect buddhas,
Come from accomplishing the genuine dharma.
Since this depends on understanding their practices,
I will explain the practices of the bodhisattvas. (B)

Now we have this great vessel of freedoms and resources, so difficult to
    obtain.
So that we may liberate ourselves and others from the ocean of samsara,
Day and night, without distraction,
To listen, contemplate, and meditate is the practice of a bodhisattva. (1)

Attachment toward our close ones stirs us up like water.
Aggression toward our enemies burns us like fire.
Dark with ignorance, we forget what to adopt or reject.
To abandon one's homeland is the practice of a bodhisattva. (2)

When we abandon negative places, the afflictions gradually diminish.
In the absence of any distraction, virtuous activity naturally increases.
Through clear awareness, certainty in the dharma arises.
To keep to solitary places is the practice of a bodhisattva. (3)

We will part from every loved one we have long associated with.
We will leave behind the wealth we have so diligently amassed.
Our consciousness, the guest, will cast away this body, the guesthouse.
To let go of this life is the practice of a bodhisattva. (4)

If you spend time with this one, the three poisons will proliferate;
The deeds of hearing, contemplating, and meditating will diminish;

And loving-kindness and compassion will become extinct.
To abandon negative friends is the practice of a bodhisattva. (5)

If you rely on this one, your faults will become exhausted
And your qualities will expand like the waxing moon.
To cherish a genuine spiritual friend
Even more than one's own body is the practice of a bodhisattva. (6)

Themselves also bound in the prison of samsara,
Whom do the worldly gods have the power to protect?
Therefore, when seeking a refuge, to go for refuge
In the three jewels that will not deceive you is the practice of a
    bodhisattva. (7)

The Sage taught that the sufferings of the lower realms,
Which are extremely difficult to bear, are the results of negative actions.
Therefore, even at the risk of one's own life,
To never commit negative actions is the practice of a bodhisattva. (8)

The pleasures of the three realms, like dewdrops on a blade of grass,
Are objects that perish in an instant.
To strive for the supreme state of liberation
That is never changing is the practice of a bodhisattva. (9)

From beginningless time, my mothers have loved me.
If they suffer, how can I worry about my own happiness?
Therefore, in order to liberate sentient beings, which are boundless,
To engender bodhichitta is the practice of a bodhisattva. (10)

All suffering, without exception, arises from the desire for one's own
    happiness.
Perfect buddhas are born from benefiting others.
Therefore, to perfectly exchange one's own happiness
For others' suffering is the practice of a bodhisattva. (11)

Even if someone, out of intense desire, steals all my wealth
Or makes another do so,

To dedicate my body, possessions, and all virtue of the three times
To them is the practice of a bodhisattva. (12)

Should someone sever my head
Even though I did not do the slightest wrong,
Through the power of compassion, to take on
Their negativity for myself is the practice of a bodhisattva. (13)

Even if some should proclaim unpleasant things
About me throughout the three-thousand-fold universe,
With a mind of loving-kindness, to speak of their good qualities
In return is the practice of a bodhisattva. (14)

Even if several people in the midst of a crowd
Should reveal my hidden faults and speak harsh words,
To hold them to be my spiritual friends
And bow to them with respect is the practice of a bodhisattva. (15)

Even if someone I cared for like my child
Should act as though I were their enemy,
Like a mother toward her child stricken with illness,
To love them even more is the practice of a bodhisattva. (16)

Even if someone my equal or lower
Should insult me influenced by pride,
To place them with respect, as if they were a guru,
At the crown of my head is the practice of a bodhisattva. (17)

Even when I am made destitute, people constantly berate me,
And grave illness and evil spirits strike me,
To take on still the suffering and misdeeds of all beings for myself
Without losing heart is the practice of a bodhisattva. (18)

Even if I become renowned and everyone pays me respect,
Or should I obtain wealth like that of Vaishravana,
To see the wealth of samsara as having no essence
And not have pride is the practice of a bodhisattva. (19)

If I do not tame the enemy of my own anger,
I may subdue external enemies, but they will still increase.
Therefore, with the army of loving-kindness and compassion,
To tame one's own mind stream is the practice of a bodhisattva. (20)

The sense pleasures are like saltwater:
However much you partake, that much your craving will increase.
Whatever objects of attachment arise,
To immediately abandon them is the practice of a bodhisattva. (21)

Whatever appears is one's own mind.
Mind is primordially free from extremes of elaboration.
Knowing this is so, to not mentally engage
The signs of perceiver and perceived is the practice of a bodhisattva. (22)

Encountering pleasurable objects
Is like seeing a rainbow in the summertime.
Although they appear beautiful and real, to see them as not being real
And relinquish attachment is the practice of a bodhisattva. (23)

The different kinds of suffering are like your child dying in a dream.
Taking confused appearances as real, how tiring!
Therefore, when meeting with adverse conditions,
To see them as confusion is the practice of a bodhisattva. (24)

Since, if you wish for enlightenment, you must give even your body away,
What is there to be said about giving material objects to others?
Therefore, to have generosity without hope of
Being paid in return is the practice of a bodhisattva. (25)

If, lacking discipline, you do not accomplish your own benefit,
Wishing to accomplish others' benefit is laughable!
Therefore, to engage in discipline
Without samsaric craving is the practice of a bodhisattva. (26)

For bodhisattvas who desire a wealth of virtue,
All harmful actions done to them are like a precious treasure.

Therefore, to practice patience that is
Without any malice toward anyone is the practice of a bodhisattva. (27)

Though the hearers and solitary realizers practice only for their own
   benefit,
They exert themselves like their hair is on fire.
Seeing this, to practice diligence, the source of qualities,
For the sake of all beings is the practice of a bodhisattva. (28)

Knowing that through superior insight endowed with thorough calm
   abiding
The mental afflictions are completely subdued,
To meditate with the concentration that perfectly goes beyond
The four formless states is the practice of a bodhisattva. (29)

Without prajna, the five paramitas
Cannot accomplish perfect enlightenment.
Therefore, to meditate on the prajna that is endowed with means
And does not conceive the three spheres is the practice of a bodhisattva. (30)

If you do not examine your own confusion,
You may, under the guise of dharma, do non-dharmic things.
Therefore, through continual examination,
To abandon one's confusion is the practice of a bodhisattva. (31)

If, under the power of the afflictive emotions,
I speak of the faults of another bodhisattva, I diminish myself.
Therefore, to not point out the faults of those who have
Entered the Mahayana is the practice of a bodhisattva. (32)

Due to honor and gain, we fight with each other
And the activities of hearing, contemplating, and meditating diminish.
Therefore, to abandon attachment to the homes of
Benefactors and loved ones is the practice of a bodhisattva. (33)

Harsh words disturb the minds of others
And cause bodhisattva activity to diminish.

Therefore, to abandon harsh words that
Are unpleasant to others is the practice of a bodhisattva. (34)

When the afflictions are habitual, they are hard to cast away with
antidotes.
Therefore, with mindfulness and attentiveness, wielding the weapon of
the antidote,
To crush the mental afflictions, such as attachment,
When they first arise is the practice of a bodhisattva. (35)

In short, in whatever you are doing,
To always, with mindfulness and attentiveness,
Ask yourself, "What is the state of my mind?"
And accomplish the benefit of others is the practice of a bodhisattva. (36)

As to these virtues, accomplished through diligence:
To dedicate them to enlightenment with the wisdom free of the three
spheres
In order to clear away the suffering
Of limitless beings is the practice of a bodhisattva. (37)

Following after the speech of the noble ones
And the meaning of what is said in the sutras, tantras, and treatises,
I have put forth these thirty-seven practices of a bodhisattva
For those who wish to practice the bodhisattva path. (c)

Because I am of inferior intellect and little training,
I do not have any poetic verse to please the learned ones.
Yet, because I have relied upon the sutras and the noble masters' speech,
I believe these practices of a bodhisattva to be without error. (d)

Nevertheless, because it is difficult for someone like me with an inferior
mind
To fathom the vastness of bodhisattva conduct,
I pray the holy ones will forgive
All faults, such as contradictions and irrelevancies. (e)

By the virtue of that, may all beings
Through the supreme bodhichitta, both ultimate and relative,
Become like the protector Avalokiteshvara,
Who does not abide in the extremes of samsara or nirvana. (F)

For the benefit of self and other, this was written by Tokmé,
a monk who follows scripture and reasoning,
at the Ngulchu Rinchen cave.

PART TWO

THE COMMENTARY

The Excellent Vase of Nectar:
The Union of Scripture and
Oral Instructions:
A Commentary on
The Thirty-Seven Practices of
a Bodhisattva

COMPOSED BY
Dzatrul Ngawang Tenzin Norbu

HOMAGE

In the vast sky of dharmakaya—the alpha-pure essence of primordial basic
space—
Unfolds the supreme mandala of your *rupakaya*, whose nature is
spontaneous presence and endowed with the five certainties.[1]
With light rays of all-pervading compassion, you open the lotuses of the
minds of those to be tamed.
To the protector Avalokiteshvara, inseparable from the supreme guru,
I bow with respect.

With your magical display as chief among *bodhisattvas*, you are a treasury
of the wisdom of supreme knowledge.
You are an ocean, a great source, of *unhindered* commentaries on the
profound key points of all yanas,
A lion among humans who always strives in *excellent* conduct with
tremendous benefit to others.
With unwavering faith, I venerate you at the crown of my head; please
care for me until enlightenment.[2]

I delight in the propagation of even a small part of the nectar essence of
the elegant explanations, deep and profound,
Which come forth from the excellent vase of your stainless voice as the
wondrous essence of your mind.
Therefore, assemblies of beings who wish to enter the house of precious
supreme liberation,
To this explanation that completely accords with all sutras, tantras, and
*upadesha*s, listen with joy![3]

INTRODUCTION

Having made the preceding homage, here I will explain the sole path that the children of the victors—the bodhisattvas—traverse, following in the footsteps of all the buddhas of the three times. This path is the single cause for accomplishing all benefit and happiness, with none left out. It is the source of all benefit and happiness within samsara and nirvana.

The teaching of this excellent wish-fulfilling jewel, a treatise on *The Thirty-Seven Practices of a Bodhisattva*, which is the heart essence of Ngulchu Chö Dzongpa[1] Gyalse Tokmé, consists of:

1. Ancillary points of the topic to be explained
    1.1 The manner of explanation by the master
    1.2 The manner of listening by the student
    1.3 How both master and student should explain and listen, respectively

These three points having been taken up at the beginning, then:

2. The actual topic to be explained
    1.4 Introduction
    1.5 The main body
    1.6 Concluding section

THE TITLE OF THE TREATISE

The Thirty-Seven Practices of a Bodhisattva

SUMMARY

Namo Guru Lokeshvaraya

Translated, this states, "I prostrate to the guru, the Lord of the World."[2]

EXTENSIVE EXPLANATION

Although he sees that all phenomena are free of coming and
   going,
He strives only for the benefit of beings.
To the protector Avalokiteshvara and the supreme guru
I continually pay homage with my three gates. (A)

He, who with all-knowing wisdom knows the extent of all knowable phenomena, sees things just as they are: suchness, the abiding nature in which
the eight extremes of elaboration—coming, going, eternalism, nihilism,
existence, nonexistence, same, [and different]—are not established anywhere. Even though this is so, he is the supreme guru who, through the
power of great love and compassion, strives only to benefit beings, teaches
me the Mahayana path, and is inseparable from noble Avalokiteshvara, the
very embodiment of the compassion of all the buddhas. To him I continually and respectfully pay homage with my three gates.

If this is applied to four points, they are the one paying homage, the one
to whom homage is paid, the way of paying homage, and the purpose of
paying homage. First, the one paying homage is the excellent bodhisattva
Ngulchu Tokmé, who first composed this treatise. The one to whom he pays
homage is the guru Avalokiteshvara, as is in accord with the topic of the text.
The way in which he pays homage is with his three gates. The reason for
which he pays homage on the relative level is so that he may be in accord with
the way of righteous ones, and to obtain the special benefits and qualities
in his mind stream. Paying homage free of the duality of subject or object is
the homage that embraces the ultimate view.

PROMISE TO COMPOSE

The sources of benefit and happiness, the perfect buddhas,
Come from accomplishing the genuine dharma.

Since this depends on understanding their practices,
I will explain the practices of the bodhisattvas. (B)

From what cause did the buddhas, the sources of temporary and ultimate happiness, arise? They arose only through practicing in accord with the dharma of the genuine Mahayana while on the path of training.

Moreover, this practice depends solely on knowing the practices, such as gathering the two accumulations, which are encompassed in the six paramitas. This consists first of engendering bodhichitta with great compassion as its root and subsequently engaging in the aspect of means,[3] such as generosity, and the aspect of wisdom—the realization that all phenomena are without self-nature. Thus, I will explain the practices of training in the attitude and conduct of the bodhisattvas for those who wish to practice the path of the Mahayana in order to obtain buddhahood as it is presented in the Mahayana—the bodhisattva *pitaka*—along with its commentaries. Who gave this explanation? Ngulchu Chö Dzongpa. What he explained is the thirty-seven practices of a bodhisattva.

In what way was it explained? It was explained in accordance with the four modes and six limits.[4] Why? It was explained in order for those of future generations who wish to practice the path of the bodhisattva to embark upon and fully complete it.

I

PRECIOUS HUMAN BIRTH

Now we have this great vessel of freedoms and resources, so
difficult to obtain.
So that we may liberate ourselves and others from the ocean
of samsara,
Day and night, without distraction,
To listen, contemplate, and meditate is the practice of a
bodhisattva. (1)

This body, which is like a vessel, was not born into the eight leisureless
states and has the ten resources. This is difficult to obtain from the point
of view of analogy, number, and cause. Now that it has been obtained, if
one wishes to accomplish the great aim of omniscience, one has the ability to do so at this time. Without letting this opportunity go to waste by
engaging in activity that has little or no meaning, day and night and in
all situations, always without distraction, listen to the profound instructions in the presence of the spiritual friend of the Mahayana, contemplate their meaning, and properly take them to heart by meditating upon
them for the sake of liberating everyone, self and other, from the ocean of
samsara.

Also, the *Entrance to the Way of a Bodhisattva* says:

It is difficult to obtain the freedoms and resources
Whereby the aims of beings may be achieved.
If I do not accomplish benefit with it now,
Later, how could I obtain the perfect resources?[1]

Not being born in the eight leisureless states, and being at leisure to practice the genuine dharma, is what is called freedom; and having no freedom refers to the eight leisureless states.

Nagarjuna said:

> Hell beings, hungry ghosts, animals,
> Barbarians, long-lived gods,
> Having wrong views, born in a time with no buddha,
> And being dumb: these are the eight leisureless states.[2]

Due to the results of each of their own previously accumulated negative karma, the beings of the three lower realms are constantly propelled into the sufferings of heat and cold, hunger and thirst, and so forth. Constantly experiencing this, they are not at leisure to practice dharma.

As for the long-lived gods, since their time is spent in a state of mental blankness, they are not at leisure to practice dharma. In outlying lands, the teachings of the Buddha are not extant, and so those born there are not at leisure to practice dharma. Non-Buddhists, or those with views that are in accord with the non-Buddhists, are not at leisure to practice dharma because their own mind streams are corrupted by such views. Born in a dark age, one will not hear even a little of the sounds of the three jewels; one is not able to practice dharma because of not recognizing what is virtuous and what is unvirtuous. If born dumb, then due to deficient cognition one is not able to practice dharma. These are the eight leisureless states.

The conducive conditions for practicing dharma are the five "self-resources," i.e., resources that are complete in relation to oneself; and the five "other-resources," i.e., resources that are complete in relation to others.

The Five Resources in Relation to Oneself

Nagarjuna said:

> Being human, born where there is dharma,[3] having intact sense
>   faculties,
> Being free of extreme karma, and having faith in the correct place.

If one does not obtain a human birth, one will not meet with the dharma; thus, having a human birth, the support, is the first resource. If one is born in outlying regions where there is no dharma, one will not meet the dharma. Having now been born in a place where there is dharma is the second, the resource of place. If one does not have all of their faculties intact, that is a hindrance to dharma. Being free from that condition is the third, the resource of possessing the capacities of the faculties. If one has extreme karma,[4] one always engages in nonvirtue and one's back is turned to the dharma. Having interest in virtuous conduct at this time is the fourth, the resource of having the special intention. If one does not have faith in the correct object, the Buddha's teachings, one's mind will not be oriented toward the dharma. Now, having the ability to turn one's mind to the dharma is the fifth, the resource of faith.

THE FIVE RESOURCES IN RELATION TO OTHERS

Nagarjuna said:

The coming of the Buddha; the Buddha having taught dharma;
The remaining of that teaching; disciples following that teaching;
And the love and compassion for the sake of others.

If one is not born in the fortunate age in which a buddha has come to this world, there will not even be the word *dharma*. Now to have been born in an era in which a buddha has come is the first, the resource of the special teacher. Even if a buddha comes, if he does not teach the dharma, there will be no benefit. The turning of the wheel of dharma in three stages, the resource of teaching the genuine dharma, is the second. Even if the dharma is taught, if the teachings diminish, it will not be of benefit. Now the period during which the teachings are extant has not yet ended; the resource of time is third. Even if the teaching remains, if one does not enter into it, it will not be of benefit. Now having the fortune of entering the gate of the teachings is the fourth resource. Even if one has entered the dharma, if one does not encounter the favorable condition of a spiritual friend, one will not understand the essence of dharma. Having done so is the resource of superior compassion, the fifth. If one investigates one's own mind stream and, accordingly, finds these eight freedoms and ten resources, totaling eighteen, perfectly complete, that is what is called the precious human birth endowed with the eighteen freedoms and resources.

The Fifth Dalai Lama said:

Now, the basis of achieving all benefit and happiness,
The vessel of freedoms and resources, has been found this once.
If I were not to go to the precious land of certainty
But return again to samsara empty-handed, my heart would rot.

These freedoms and resources are difficult to obtain from the point of view of number, cause, condition, and analogy.

BEING DIFFICULT TO OBTAIN FROM THE POINT OF VIEW OF CAUSE

The *Entrance to the Middle Way* states:

The cause of the higher realms is nothing other than discipline.

There is much nonvirtue performed by sentient beings, and the virtue they perform is little. Obtaining this life in which one has the dharma has come about due to its cause: discipline and the power of accumulating much merit.

BEING DIFFICULT TO OBTAIN FROM THE POINT OF VIEW OF CONDITION

The cause is obtaining the precious human birth. The condition is being accepted by the spiritual friend, the guru. If one can practice the genuine dharma, the means, one can definitely obtain buddhahood in one life and one body. Meeting with such profound key instructions is extremely difficult.

BEING DIFFICULT TO OBTAIN FROM THE POINT OF VIEW OF ANALOGY

The support of this precious human birth is like the analogy of the meeting of a blind turtle with a single yoke on a great ocean.
Shantideva said:

Like a turtle's neck poking through
A yoke's hole on the churning ocean,
It is taught that a human life is very difficult to obtain.[5]

THE SPECIAL CONTEMPLATION FROM THE POINT OF VIEW OF NUMBER

If one examines the quantity and the levels of sentient beings that exist, obtaining a human birth is just barely possible. Accordingly, the hell beings are as many as the particles of dust in a vast land. Hungry ghosts are as numerous as the grains of sand in the Ganges. Animals are as many as the dregs from making chang.[6] Jealous gods are as many as the gusts in a wind storm. It is taught that the gods and humans are only as many as the motes of dust on top of a fingernail. Generally, the bodies of the higher realms are rare. Thus, the freedoms and resources of a human birth are also rare. However one thinks about it, if one should wonder about the purpose of obtaining this human birth that has the six elements[7] and is certainly difficult to obtain: it is only through relying on this support that all the buddhas of the three times arrived at the primordial state. If we do not obtain it, there is no way to have even a little of the result of the bliss of the higher realms, let alone liberation.

The Second Buddha, Padmakara, also said:

This precious human birth of freedoms and resources is difficult to
obtain.
Whether examined in terms of cause, condition, analogy, or number,
Obtaining it is certainly difficult; all the victors relied on it to go
beyond.
Thus, think of the difficulties of finding the freedoms and resources
And, day and night, without leisure, practice the genuine dharma.

Even if all the supports of these outer freedoms and resources come together and one actually obtains that which is so difficult to obtain, still, [consider] the inner leisureless states. The omniscient Gyalwa Longchen Rabjam's *Wish-Fulfilling Treasury*[8] says that it is very important for those who desire the genuine dharma to examine in detail whether their mind stream is going to waste with respect to the eight leisureless states that are temporary conditions and the eight leisureless states of the mind of the cut-off class.[9]

Likewise, the *Wish-Fulfilling Treasury* states:

Agitation by the five poisons; ignorance; possession by maras;
Laziness; the erupting of a great ocean of negative deeds;

Enslavement; no protection from fear; and pretending to be dharmic:
These are the eight leisureless states that are temporary conditions.

Also:

Being tightly fettered; extremely negative conduct;
Not being dissatisfied with samsara; having no faith whatsoever;
Unvirtuous conduct; having a mind free of dharma;
And violating the vows and the *samayas*:
These are the eight leisureless states of the mind of the cut-off class.

THE EIGHT LEISURELESS STATES THAT ARE TEMPORARY CONDITIONS

Those who have the five mental afflictions that are very coarse, such as attachment and aggression toward friends and enemies, may occasionally give rise to the wish to practice the dharma genuinely, but if their mind stream is overtaken by the five poisons, they will likely not practice dharma. This is the first leisureless state that is a temporary condition.

Those who are very ignorant, even if they enter the gate of dharma, cannot understand even a little of dharma's meaning; they do not have the fortune to practice dharma with their three gates. This is the second.

If one takes on a teacher who teaches incorrect views and conduct—a mara[10] of the teachings—one's mind becomes perverted and is contradictory to true dharma. This is the third.

Even if someone desires to train in the dharma, if they are lazy, without even the slightest diligence, they do not practice dharma due to falling prey to the habit of procrastination. This is the fourth.

Even if someone has diligence, if they are obscured by negativity that does not allow good qualities to arise in their mind stream, their great ocean of negative karma erupts forth; they do not understand that the negative karma of their own actions is a weapon turned on themselves. Not developing confidence in the dharma is the fifth.

If someone is enslaved by another, there is no freedom. Even if they desire to practice dharma, they are not allowed to practice because of being under another's control. This is the sixth.

And if someone enters the dharma in order to have protection from the fear of not being able to obtain food and clothing or of someone harming them, then because they have no conviction in the dharma and have old habitual tendencies, they engage in non-dharmic activity. This is the seventh.

Pretending to be dharmic while only having concern for this life, one distorts the dharma as a way to obtain respect, renown, honor, and gain and is separated from the path to liberation. This is the eighth.

These are the states that do not allow leisure to practice dharma.

THE EIGHT LEISURELESS STATES OF THE MIND OF THE CUT-OFF CLASS

Tightly bound by the fetters of this life—children, wealth, enjoyments, and so forth—one is distracted from diligent effort and does not have time to practice dharma. This is the first leisureless state of the mind of the cut-off class.

Because of one's negative mind stream, there is not even a sesame seed's worth of good character and one's conduct shows no sign of improvement. Even if one meets with a genuine spiritual guide, it will be difficult to follow the genuine path. This is the second.

If no fear arises toward the faults of samsara in general, toward the lower realms in particular, or toward the sufferings of this life and so forth, whatever they may be, the cause of entering the dharma will never arise. This is the third.

If someone does not have even a little bit of faith in the genuine dharma or the guru, then the entrance to the teachings is blocked, and they will not enter the path of liberation. This is the fourth.

If someone enjoys engaging in unvirtuous, negative deeds, their three gates will not be at peace. Being devoid of any positive qualities, they are turned away from the dharma. This is the fifth.

If the dharma's good qualities, virtue, and so forth are not evident to someone, then they will have no interest in the dharma. They will be like a dog that has dirt placed in front of him. Good qualities will not arise in their mind stream; this is the sixth.

If, having entered the common vehicle, someone breaks their vows and becomes cut off from generating a good intention, they cannot be liberated from the leisureless states and can only go to the lower realms. This is the seventh.

Having entered into the uncommon vehicle of mantra, if someone's samaya with their guru and dharma brothers and sisters declines, then due to such behavior, which brings all involved to ruin, they will be cut off from the good fortune of attaining the *siddhis*. This is the eighth.

These states are called "distant from genuine dharma" and "the dimming of the lamp of liberation."

If one does not examine these sixteen leisureless states well, though one may appear to practice dharma and to have the freedoms and resources intact in this polluted age, then, falling under the power of these leisureless states, even with intention of practicing dharma, they will only turn away from the genuine path. This being so, the conduct of always carefully examining one's mind stream is important.

The incomparable Atisha said:

> The body replete with the freedoms and resources
> That is extremely difficult to obtain has been obtained.
> Since it will be difficult to obtain again,
> Through effort in practice, make it meaningful.

Gyalwa Tsongkhapa said:

> If you understand the difficulty of attaining it, you will not remain idle.
> One who sees its great significance would be devastated to spend it without purpose.

Geshe Chen-ngawa, never sleeping, only engaged in virtue. Geshe Tönpa said to him, "Son, if you do not get some rest, you will endanger your health." Chen-ngawa replied, "My body is perfect now. When I consider the difficulty of obtaining the freedoms and resources of this body, there is no time to rest." He did 900 million recitations of Akshobhya.[11] Because of that, we can be certain that he never had time to sleep in his life. Likewise, it is very important to make this precious support with its freedoms a meaningful one. Right now, moreover, do not let the path go to waste. Always, day and night, you should engage in the dharma with your three gates. Like that, the practice of the bodhisattvas is to make meaningful the freedoms and resources of this body that is difficult to find.

2

ABANDONING ONE'S HOMELAND

Attachment toward our close ones stirs us up like water.
Aggression toward our enemies burns us like fire.
Dark with ignorance, we forget what to adopt or reject.
To abandon one's homeland is the practice of a bodhisattva. (2)

If we stay in our own homeland when practicing dharma, we focus on close ones such as our friends with whom we are affectionate and our parents with whom we have great mutual love and care. Through that, our attachment stirs us up like water. When we take others with whom we have mutual ill feelings to be enemies, aggression arises like fire and burns away the virtue that has been accumulated in our own and others' mind streams. The arising of ignorance, like thick darkness, makes us forget and causes the decline of our mindfulness and attentiveness regarding the virtue that is appropriate to adopt and the nonvirtue to be rejected. One should abandon one's homeland, which is of the nature of so many faults.

The *Request of Adhyasaya Sutra* also states:

It is best to go a hundred leagues away
From any place with busyness and struggle.
One should not stay even for an instant
Wherever one has the mental afflictions.

Accordingly, if you remain in the land of your birth, or a place that promotes self-fixation, the strength of the three poisons will increase. In that land to which one is attached, one clings to one's house, and seductive friends flatter us. Objects that fetter us bind us tightly. Desire and attachment carry us down the stream of samsara, churning like water. Not only that, we bear grudges toward enemies of the past and worry about those of the future, and aggression arises ceaselessly toward the enemies of the present. Practice the completely perfect dharma by abandoning your homeland. If you remain there and do not separate from those with whom you are close, there will be happiness, pleasure, sickness, and death; you will not have time,[1] you will have no leisure, and, being tied up in every second, you will not be allowed to practice dharma. Turning your back on your homeland to which you are so closely connected and staying in a place where there are no friends and acquaintances is the only profound way.

Lord Atisha said:

> Overturn the prison of maras, one's homeland.
> Cut the fetters of non-dharmic action.
> Escape from the friends you love, from the enemies you hate,
> And from the land of negative karma, anger, and attachment.

Lord Milarepa said:

> One's homeland is the prison of maras.
> Gaining freedom is hard; quickly escape.
> Youthful companions are female maras:[2]
> They'll surely deceive you; be cautious of them.
> Sensory pleasures are the noose of maras;
> They'll surely bind you; let go of attachment!

Gyalwa Longchenpa said:

> Worldly deeds are like an elephant entering the mud.
> Sentiment for our relatives is like a prison guard.
> The enjoyments of this life are like an old dog gnawing on a bone.
> Ignorant negative conduct is like a blind person on the edge of a cliff.
> The afflictions—the five poisons—are like playing with a poisonous
>   snake.
> Attachment to the six sense objects is like a fly stuck in sap.
> Generate fear and cherish casting them far away.

Götsangpa said:

> One's homeland is a storehouse of the five poisons.
> It's the cause of the arising of attachment and aggression, so
>   unbearable.
> Knowing well that I must leave this behind,
> I will roam in empty lands free of people.

It is very important to give up the friends and relatives of one's homeland. Therefore, to give up one's homeland, the root of attachment and aggression, is the practice of a bodhisattva.

3

RELYING ON SOLITARY PLACES

When we abandon negative places, the afflictions gradually
   diminish.
In the absence of any distraction, virtuous activity naturally
   increases.
Through clear awareness, certainty in the dharma arises.
To keep to solitary places is the practice of a bodhisattva. (3)

Even if you are practicing the dharma purely, doing so in your homeland or in
a place with bad qualities is contrary to dharma by its very nature. If you keep
to places of solitude, then all the afflictions, such as attachment and aggression, will gradually diminish and subside, and pure discipline will dawn.
Without the fault of distractions and busyness—like engaging in the respon-
sibilities of business and farming for the sake of yourself and others, such as
close ones and relatives—virtuous activity of the three gates, such as diligence in the yoga of one-pointed *samadhi*, will naturally increase. When you
obtain mental stillness, the mind becomes workable and awareness becomes
clear. Then, through your examining and analyzing dharma's meaning with
prajna, certainty arises. In this way, keeping to places of solitude has many
qualities, such as increasing the practices of the three trainings.

THE CHARACTERISTICS OF A SOLITARY PLACE

The *Ornament of the Sutras* states:

The place of practice of any intelligent one
Has good facilities,[1] is a good environment,

Is a good location, has good companions,
And produces the qualities of blissful practice.

Accordingly, it is said that one should seek out a place where it is easy to obtain alms; is a good environment with no thieves and robbers; is a good location without floods and disease; has good companions who practice in accord with the dharma; and is a place that, without causing one to have trepidation toward meditative concentration, produces the qualities of blissful practice.

The *Entrance to the Way of a Bodhisattva* states:

Thus, wearied by your craving,
Give rise to joy in solitude.[2]

Lord Atisha said:

Until you obtain stability, seek out deep solitary forests, since stability is harmed by busyness.

Rigdzin Jikme Lingpa said:

Not attached to things obtained, like the wind or a *garuda*,
Like a deer who stays in isolation,
Do not become agitated by frivolous conduct.

The Fifth Dalai Lama said:

Through delusion and distraction in your births until now,
You wasted your lives—made them meaningless and empty.
Now, in a sublime place isolated from worldly busyness,
Delight fully in practicing this way.

If you stay in isolation, you will naturally be separated from all the desires and deeds of this life. As a matter of course, you will engage only in virtue. In that way, seeking out solitary places that are in accord with the source of all qualities is the practice of a bodhisattva.

4

REMEMBERING IMPERMANENCE

We will part from every loved one we have long associated with.
We will leave behind the wealth we have so diligently
    amassed.
Our consciousness, the guest, will cast away this body, the
    guesthouse.
To let go of this life is the practice of a bodhisattva. (4)

However many relatives—such as your parents, whom you have associated with for a long time from birth until death—and close friends you may have, when death comes they will dispense with you and you will also dispense with them. It is certain that everyone will part. At the time of death, you will not carry with you even a little bit of the wealth that you amassed with diligence and great pains, paying no heed to suffering or negative deeds. Nor will it follow after you. Even while you do not mentally forsake it, you will give it up physically. Beings are like a hair pulled out of butter.[1] Not only that, you should contemplate how when consciousness, the guest, casts away the guesthouse—the body that is intact from birth and composed of bones and flesh—it will go friendless and alone to an unfamiliar place. From now on, letting go of all enemies to subdue, friends to protect, harvests, profits, the deeds of this life that has many faults due to petty-mindedness, and so forth, give rise to the mind that strives for the benefit of the next life.

The sutras make statements such as:

The three realms of samsara are impermanent like a cloud in
    autumn;
The birth and death of beings is like watching a dance.

Impermanence can be illustrated by many similes; it applies to the entire outer world and all of the inhabitants contained within it. Thus, remember and meditate upon impermanence.

First, from the *Jataka Tales*:

> First was the night of entering the womb.
> From that point, we enter the ways of this world,
> And until we reach the next life,
> We get closer and closer to the Lord of Death's feet.

In that way, you should understand that not even an instant of this life will remain; like a waterfall, it passes on.

The sutras state:

> We do not know which will come first,
> Tomorrow or the next world.
> Do not strive for the sake of tomorrow;
> It is proper to strive for the sake of the next life.

The Vinaya states:

> Compared with offering the midday meal along with gifts to my retinue—Shariputra, Maudgalyana, and a hundred like them— remembering, for an instant, the impermanence of composite phenomena is supreme.

In the beginning, remembering impermanence is the cause of entering the dharma; in the middle, it is the condition for compelling one toward virtue; and finally, it aids in one's realizing the equality of phenomena.

Second, there are also many specific ways to meditate on impermanence. One can meditate in terms of the three roots, the nine reasons, and the three resolves.

The three roots are contemplating the certainty of death, contemplating the unpredictability of the time of death, and contemplating that at the time of death nothing other than the dharma will be of help.

The three reasons for the first, the certainty of death, are that there is no one, without exception, who previously lived who did not die; the body is composite; and moment by moment, this life is being spent.

The three reasons for the second, the unpredictability of death, are that this life is uncertain; the body is without essence; and there are many conditions for death.

The three reasons for the third root, that at the time of death nothing other than the dharma will be of help, are that the spiritual friend will not be of benefit; wealth will not be of benefit; and even your own body will not be of benefit.

These sets of three reasons altogether make nine. These were not elaborated upon.

The three resolves are the resolve that, since death is certain, one must practice the dharma, which is certain to be of benefit at the time of death; the resolve that, since the time of death is unpredictable, from now on, one must practice dharma; and the resolve that, since nothing other than dharma will be of benefit at the time of death, one must only practice dharma without getting thrown by the power of physical enjoyments and relations.

The sutras state:

If all the buddhas, the solitary realizers,
And the hearers of the buddhas
Have relinquished their bodies,
What needs to be said of ordinary beings?

The *Entrance to the Way of a Bodhisattva* states:

"At least today, I will not die."
Being content with such words is irrational.[2]

The Great One from Uddiyana [Padmasambhava] said:

The appearances of this life are like last night's dream.
Sensory pleasures and riches are like an illusory banquet.
Meaningless deeds are like a ripple in the water.

Padampa Sangye said:

In the midst of distraction, the mara of death will take you.
People of Dingri, practice now!

And:

> Abandoning all possessions, beings, whoever they may be, should
> be free of activity and without attachment to anything.

Tsongkhapa said:

> There is no time to spare, while we have the freedoms and resources,
>   difficult to obtain:
> By cultivating your mind, turn away from the fancies of this life.

Lord Milarepa said:

> Having great fear of the eight leisureless states,
> I meditated on impermanence and the faults of samsara
> And wholeheartedly put my trust in the refuges, the three jewels.
> I developed persistence in the dharma of karma, cause and effect.
> I purified my mind stream through bodhichitta, the means,
> And cut the stream of habitual tendencies.
> I have realized whatever appears are illusions.
> I have no fear of the lower three realms.

Götsangpa said:

> Cutting the rope of attachment to one's homeland,
> Unsticking the glue that binds one to relatives, and
> Cutting through attachment to wealth:
> These three will happen if you meditate upon impermanence and
>   death.

The Fifth Dalai Lama also said:

> Without any certain time of day, month, or year,
> We can see that young and old all die without set order.
> You with the water-bubble eyes,[3] whose time of death is set,
> Look at this well!

Karmapa Rolpe Dorje said:

At the time when the Lord of Death comes to you,
It is difficult to have a happy mind.
Not knowing where you will go in your next lives,
Now is the time for you to carefully consider this.

An ornament among the flock of Gampopa's close disciples, a layperson named Druptop Chöyung, offered a bolt of cloth and requested teachings, but Gampopa would not give them. Again, he requested with great fervor, and Gampopa grabbed the disciple's arm with his hand and said, "I will die and you will also die!" Three times he repeated only this. Then the lama also said, "I have no other practice than that. You should meditate on this." He promised to practice this instruction. It is said the man became a *siddha* by meditating in that way.

The *Great Parinirvana Sutra* states:

Among all thoughts, the thoughts of death and impermanence are supreme.

Thus, all the sutras, treatises, and upadeshas say that relinquishing this life by meditating on impermanence is the supreme path. Doing so, one will give up all worldly attachments. It is what urges one to instantly traverse all the experiences and realizations. It is the foundation of all dharma. It is the sole indispensable dharma that is the root of all qualities.

Dromtönpa said:

If you do not relinquish this life by meditating on impermanence, nothing you do will be in accord with dharma. You will not go beyond the eight worldly concerns. If you do relinquish this life, you will be free from the eight worldly concerns.

The Great Lord of Bodhisattvas [Ngulchu Tokmé] said:

If you will not tame your mind by staying in solitary places
Without working to tame enemies or to protect friends,
Without serving masters, and without servants looking after you,
Then what is there for you to do, mani-reciters?[4]

As it is said here and elsewhere, to relinquish this life by meditating on impermanence is the practice of a bodhisattva.

5

ABANDONING BAD FRIENDS

If you spend time with this one, the three poisons will proliferate;
The deeds of hearing, contemplating, and meditating will
    diminish;
And loving-kindness and compassion will become extinct.
To abandon negative friends is the practice of a bodhisattva. (5)

When you spend time with just any friends and acquaintances, the afflictions that cut the life force of liberation—the three poisons—will proliferate. All the deeds of the genuine dharma, such as hearing, contemplating, and meditating—the main causes of accomplishing liberation—will naturally diminish. Negative friends, unvirtuous spiritual teachers, and so forth, who never engage in any positive deeds such as bodhichitta, loving-kindness, and compassion—the roots of the Mahayana path—are like dangerous beasts; knowing this, abandon them.

The *Udanavarga* also states:

Do not spend time with wicked people.
If someone who is virtuous follows
An unvirtuous person,
Concern will arise that they have done nonvirtue,
And their bad reputation will spread.

The *Application of Mindfulness Sutra* states:

The basis of attachment, aggression, and ignorance is negative friends. View them as a poisonous tree.

Accordingly, there are two types of negative friends: spiritual teachers who teach the wrong path and negative companions.

As for the first type: If you meet and spend time with anyone who follows the path of mistaken view and conduct, such as an unvirtuous spiritual teacher, your mind stream will be overtaken, both this life and the next will decline, and you will be fundamentally mistaken about the path of all positive qualities and good things. Even if you have virtuous teachers who show the path of the hearers and solitary realizers, you will deviate from the bodhisattva path and become separated from it. Do not follow such teachings.[1] In particular, dishonest charlatans, being mostly hypocritical, are masters of deception. If, because this is not fully understood, these teachers are not investigated and examined, all accumulated virtues of the faithful ones who go to them for teachings, along with their human lives endowed with the freedoms and resources, will go to waste.

As the Great One from Uddiyana said:

Not examining the guru is like drinking poison.

As for the second type: Because of negative companions, mental afflictions and the three poisons increase. One will engage in nonvirtue and negative karma, and the activities of hearing, contemplating, and meditating—such as discipline—will be hindered and will naturally decline. Not only that, you must abandon all negative friends who completely destroy all of the positive dharmas that you have previously accumulated, such as the roots of the Mahayana: loving-kindness, compassion, and bodhichitta.

It is said:

If you associate with friends who are frenzied, you will be carried away by distraction.
If you associate with greedy friends, you will chase after profit.
If you associate with friends who wish for worldly happiness, this life will pass you by.
If you associate with friends who are engaged in many activities, meditative concentration will fade.

Dromtönpa asked Atisha, "Of all the enemies, which is the worst?" Atisha replied, "Destructive, negative companions are the worst." Again,

Dromtönpa asked, "What is the greatest condition for contradicting the vows?" Atisha replied, "People who are objects of desire[2] and liquor."

Potowa said:

> If we listen to negative friends and act in accord with their conduct, we will make our [lives] meaningless and will be mistaken in the affairs of this life and the next.

Sharawa said:

> Since the root of the kleshas is people who are objects of desire, do not associate with them.

Abandoning negative friends while understanding they are like an infectious disease or a deadly enemy is the bodhisattvas' way of abandoning negative friends.

6

Relying on Good Friends

If you rely on this one, your faults will become exhausted
And your qualities will expand like the waxing moon.
To cherish a genuine spiritual friend
Even more than one's own body is the practice of a
bodhisattva. (6)

If you approach or rely on this kind of friend, the faults within your mind stream—such as attachment and aggression—will become exhausted. All the good qualities such as hearing, contemplating, and meditating, together with loving-kindness, compassion, and bodhichitta, will increase more and more, like the waxing of the moon. In both thought and deed, rely properly on a spiritual friend.

Also, the *Condensed Perfection of Wisdom Sutra* states:

Excellent students who have respect for the guru
Should always rely on wise gurus.
Why is that so? It is from them that the qualities of wisdom arise.

In all of the sutras and tantras, it is never said that buddhahood can be accomplished without relying on a master. Not only that, there is no one in this life who has attained the paths and levels of the spiritual path through the pride of their own concocted way of seeing the dharma. Right now everyone, ourselves and others, are the same as a friendless blind man lost in an empty field. Just like the metaphor of failing to obtain treasure from an island of jewels because of not relying on the captain, one should respectfully rely on spiritual teachers and friends since they are the ones who actually know the path of omniscience and liberation.

Potowa said:

> Without a teacher, how can we who have just come from the lower realms go to a place we have never been before?

EXAMINING THE CHARACTERISTICS OF A GURU

The Faults of a Guru to Be Abandoned

The *Inner Tantras* states:

> Having great pride yet without understanding,
> Following after those who are ignorant,
> Discouraging others through harsh speech,
> Engaging in wrong paths,
> Having great pride even though unlearned—
> An unexamined guru becomes the disciple's mara.

Although they do not have even a small part of the good qualities of hearing and meditation in their mind streams, [faulty spiritual teachers] give their high social class, and so forth, as a reason [that they are qualified masters]. Saying, "I'm such and such a bodhisattva," they have the conceit that they are protected by being of a high caste, just like Brahmins. Furthermore, although they are not beyond the mental capacity of ordinary people, they say they are something they are not and vie with siddhas in their conduct. Some consider themselves to be great, even if they have done only a little hearing and meditation. Due to the gain and respect they receive, they have inflated ideas about themselves. Being haughty and prideful, such stubborn and foolish ones do not see the qualities of holy beings. If anyone should encounter such a false spiritual friend who gets angry, uses many hostile words, and, in particular, cuts the lifeline of compassion and loving-kindness, then, just like following a crazy guide, one who has faith in them will exhaust their life's accumulated virtue. They will be deceived about having found the freedoms of a precious human birth, like mistaking a poisonous snake for the shadow of a tree.

The Characteristics of a Guru One Should Seek Out

The guru to be relied upon should have four characteristics. The *Ornament of the Sutras* states:

> One who is suitable to be adopted as a teacher has these two:
> Vast knowledge and eradication of all doubts.
> They also teach the path of the bodhisattvas and
> Have perfected the accumulations.

A genuine teacher has, without delusion, widely studied the essential points of the sutras, tantras, treatises, the three vows, and so on. Through complete understanding of the intended meaning of those—the good qualities of realization and abandoning what should be abandoned, and so forth—they are able to cut through the doubts of others. The deeds of a wise being are performed with a mind that is saturated with love for all sentient beings, like a mother with a single child; thus they are suitable to be relied upon. They teach that the nature of both the thoroughly afflicted and the thoroughly purified is suchness. Furthermore, you should rely on someone who attracts fortunate disciples through the four ways of magnetizing: generosity, pleasant speech, meaningful conduct, and acting with consistency in words and deeds.

For example, if an ordinary tree in a forest of sandalwood should fall, gradually that tree too will take on a nice fragrance. Similarly, if one relies upon a wise being endowed with good qualities, all of the qualities of that teacher will spread to the student. As it is said:

> An ordinary log that rolls about
> In the vast forest of Malaya
> Becomes saturated with the smell of sandalwood;
> Accordingly, rely upon someone with good qualities, and follow them.

RELYING UPON A GURU THROUGH ATTITUDE AND CONDUCT

Cultivation of Faith, the Root

As it is said in the sutras:

First give rise to the preliminaries, which are like a mother.

In order for a noble guru to guide beings to be tamed through means, the guru's relatively appearing deeds, their conduct and so forth, appear to be the same as everyone else's. However, from the viewpoint of definitive reality, their conduct conflicts with everyone else's because they have entered into buddhahood. Since whatever action they exhibit is intended solely to be harmonious with the mind streams of those to be tamed, it is superior. Just like a mother would be with her only child, the master is patient with students who deviate from the path and all of those who cause difficulties. With a sense of devotion, one should consider such a guru to be inseparable from an actual buddha. Whatever actions they do, consider them to be good; whatever they say, with deep interest and respect, accept it as unmistaken and revere it; [in their presence], quickly rise, bow, and attend them; speak to them with a mind of loving care; without being contented, look at them again and again.

The *Gandavyuha Sutra* states:

Do not ever feel contented when looking at the spiritual friend. Why? Because it is very difficult to have the opportunity to see a genuine spiritual friend. It is difficult for one to appear, and it is difficult to meet one.

The *Sutra on the Ten Dharmas* states:

People who are without faith
Do not develop positive dharmas,
Just like a seed that is burned by fire is scorched
And does not give rise to a sprout.

Faith is very important!

Recollecting the Kindness of the Guru

Despite the compassion of the countless buddhas who came before, they did not have the power to protect us, so we have been left until now in samsara, the great ocean of suffering. In this present time of the Buddha's teaching, many accomplished ones have come; however, we have not become the object of their compassionate sight. We have not even had the fortune of meeting them in person. And now, even though we have obtained a human birth, in this time of the rampant spread of the five degenerations, we have only become controlled by nonvirtue. In this time of ignorance of what to adopt and what to reject, through their consideration of boundless compassion, they have come, in the form of a person who is compatible with each individual's capacity, and have taken care of us with skillful means and wisdom. Since the spiritual friend teaches the unmistaken profound, genuine dharma, meeting them is actually no different from meeting a true buddha in person. From our vantage point, their kindness is even greater than a buddha's, beyond any measure.

The *Flower Ornament Sutra* says:

> The spiritual friend protects us from the lower realms. The spiritual friend is like a rower who liberates us from the great river of samsara.

Panchen Chögyen also said:

> For beings of this polluted age who are difficult to tame
> And could not be tamed by the countless buddhas who came
>   before,
> They are the compassionate protector
> Who teaches the excellent path of the *sugatas* as it is.

The sutras state:

> Rely on the spiritual friend through respect,
> Material offerings, attending, and practicing.

The three ways of pleasing the master:

In the supreme form of service, one acts with perseverance and endurance to bring into their experience all the dharma that is taught and accomplishes it completely.

The *Jataka Tales* states:

The offering of repaying benefit
Is to practice in accord with their instructions.

The middling service of body and speech is attending the guru—putting one's body, speech, and mind in their service. Since it is the unmistaken path of accumulation, you should strive to do whatever you can, even down to sweeping their room. Even if the guru should scold you and wear an expression of anger, you should consider that scolding you and criticizing your faults is done to tame you. Since there is no way to repay their kindness, with one-pointed respect think, "I go for refuge!"[1] When they are in a more peaceful mood, confess and renew your commitments. Never sit in the presence of the guru—stand; ask about their health; offer them what they need and wish and so forth. If you are their attendant when they travel, do not walk in front of them, as you will show your back to them. Do not follow behind them because you will tread on their footsteps. Do not walk to their right because that is treading in a high position. Instead, respectfully walk on their left side and a little bit behind. If you need to go ahead or behind for any reason, ask for permission. Do not trample on their seat or horse. Abandon wearing flashy garments, saying unpleasant things, using rash speech, lying, and a mind of indifference. You should train in conduct that is respectful.

As Drom Rinpoche [Dromtönpa] said:

If you do what the guru says with meditative focus, then without having to do anything, you will accomplish everything.

The least of the ways to serve the guru is to please them by freely offering them material things: food, wealth, gifts, and so forth. Even though the guru does not actually care about such material things, they act, on a relative level, as though they are pleasing in order for those to be tamed to perfect the accumulation of merit.

The tantras state:

Such generosity
Is a continuous offering to all the buddhas.
That offering is the accumulation of merit,
And from such accumulation, supreme siddhi will come.

In order to accomplish the immense accumulation of merit, one should offer whatever cherished possessions they have. Not only that, if there is something unsuitable or too difficult to achieve, if [the guru] nonetheless says to do it, then thinking, "This is undoubtedly for my benefit," you should engage in what they tell you, without any hesitation. If there is something that you cannot do and do not fully accomplish it, the *Fifty Verses [of Relying on a Guru]* states:

If you are not able to accomplish something,
Purify through explaining that shortcoming.

It is inappropriate to think it is unnecessary to explain and purify well one's lack of accomplishing the guru's instruction.

Of the three ways to serve the guru, it is said that mainly through the offering of practice they will be pleased.

Langthangpa said:

The guru will be pleased by your practice. Cease the hardship of [other means of] accumulating merit.

Nevertheless, if you train from the least of these ways on up, all will turn out well. Through your training in these ways of relying upon the guru through the three ways of pleasing them, all of the qualities of realization and the abandonment of what is to be abandoned will gradually increase like grass growing in the summer.

The life story of Shri Sambhava states:

The enlightenment of the buddhas is obtained through serving the spiritual friend.

An explanatory tantra states:

> The merit of offering to a single hair of the guru is greater
> Than the offerings made to all the buddhas of the three times.

Since there is none higher than the supreme guru, who is the field of accumulation of merit, you should make offerings to them with exertion.

The previous bodhisattvas of India such as Dharmodgata, Sadaprarudita, and the great pandita Naropa, and those in the Land of Snow—the fathers and sons of the Kadampa lineage, Marpa, Milarepa, Gampopa, and so forth, the great holy beings of the Kagyu—first, at the time of relying on their spiritual teachers, ignored all hardship and exhaustion, without any regard even for their own lives and bodies. Due to the power of their excellent and marvelous way of relying on the spiritual teacher, it did not take them long to master the view; they went to the perfect state. Through their serving under them in that way, the good qualities developed.

The *Accomplishment of Wisdom*[2] states:

> Without a rower,
> A boat cannot get to the other side.
> Even if one has completely perfected all good qualities,
> Without a guru, liberation is not possible.

Right now, we do not now know how to rely properly on a genuine guru; or even if we do know, we do not put it into practice effectively. We are not able to train in the view and conduct. We think that we equal them; never mind seeing them as a buddha. Having only the contempt of belittling them, moreover, we audaciously think we have excellent experience and realization and talk much about our having an extremely high realization. This is like trying to find butter in sand, or like a blooming lotus in a fire.[3]

Dromtönpa asked Lord Atisha:

> "In Tibet, why is it that there are many who meditate, but the good qualities do not arise in very many of them?" Atisha replied, "Since they have the thought that the guru is ordinary, how could such qualities arise?"

Tibetan teachers asked Atisha with great fervor:

> "Atisha, please give us pith instructions." He replied, "Hey, hey!
> Listen to me, this is the excellent view: Faith! Faith!"

Dromtönpa also said:

> Day and night, rely on the condition, the spiritual friend. Associate with the excellent fortress, the genuine friend of virtue.

The Great One from Uddiyana said:

> If you don't understand the guru to be a buddha,
> Their blessings will not liberate you.
> While thinking of their qualities, supplicate the guru.

The Good Qualities of Properly Relying on the Guru in This Way

It is said:

> The benefits are that the victors will be happy; the spiritual friend
>   will be pleased;
> You will not fall to the lower realms; karma and afflictions will not
>   overtake you;
> Through the increase of good qualities, the temporary and ultimate
>   goals will be accomplished;
> And the qualities of buddhahood will shine forth.

Considering the benefits as stated, it is important to practice the completely pure way of relying on the guru.

The Faults of Improperly Relying on the Guru

It is said:

> If one should rely on the guru in a mistaken way,
> Ignorant at the time of death, they will burn in the hottest hell;

The good qualities will not arise; or if they have arisen, they will decline;
And they will have negative companions—spiritual guides will remove these faults.

When considering the meaning of this, one becomes very focused because of the fear of these faults. In the three realms there is none more powerful and kind than the guru. Therefore, the advantages of relying on a guru and the risks of not relying on one are very great.

The Fifth Dalai Lama said:

From the perspective of your own errant and mistaken mind,
All of your faults appear as the deeds of the guru.
Through certainty that your own heart is rotten in its depths,
Understand that they are your own faults and relinquish them like poison.

Also:

Whatever actions the guru does, regard them as excellent, with pure vision.
Whatever the guru commands, devotedly accomplish it.
Whatever the guru may do, see it as a profound vital point that turns to dharma.
For then, that which you wish, the root of benefit and happiness, will be accomplished.

Just as the roots of all dharma texts, the Sanskrit works whose titles are placed at the beginning [of their Tibetan translations], are examined,[4] once you have made the decision with regard to the risks and benefits, you should cherish the guru. This way of relying on the spiritual friend is the practice of a bodhisattva.

7

GOING FOR REFUGE

Themselves also bound in the prison of samsara,
Whom do the worldly gods have the power to protect?
Therefore, when seeking a refuge, to go for refuge
In the three jewels that will not deceive you is the practice of
  a bodhisattva. (7)

They themselves having also entered the prison of samsara that is very difficult to escape and being powerfully bound by the tight shackles of karma and mental afflictions, the source of all suffering, what power do the great worldly gods have to protect from this? They do not have the slightest ability to protect us.

However, if you seek refuge in the special object, it will never deceive you. Go for refuge, completely entrusting yourself to the three jewels, which undeniably have the power to protect everyone, self and others, from all the fears of samsara and nirvana.

Further, the *Seventy Stanzas on Refuge* states:

The Buddha, dharma, and sangha
Are the refuges for those who desire liberation.

Since it is not possible to be liberated from the fear of samsara and nirvana without relying on the power of the Buddha, the method of going for refuge in those who seek liberation consists of (1) the cause of going for refuge; (2) the object of going for refuge; (3) the method of going for refuge; (4) the commitments for going for refuge; and (5) the benefits of going for refuge.

THE CAUSE OF GOING FOR REFUGE: THE PAIN OF FEAR

If we did not have any fears and had the power to attain enlightenment, there would be no need to seek refuge. However, it is not like that for us now. Since beginningless time we have been oppressed by the slothful mind of ignorance, bound by the noose of karma and mental afflictions, and punished by birth, old age, sickness, and death.

The torturous suffering in the city of the lower realms, like a whirling firebrand, must be experienced without break. Because of that, one has fear and terror. Through confident faith in the three jewels, which have the power to protect from such fear, one has the mental state of complete trust and confidence.

TRUSTING REFUGE IN THE SPECIAL OBJECT

Without ever deceiving, the three precious jewels undeniably have the ability to protect everyone, self and others, from all fears of samsara and nirvana. They are a refuge from the fears of samsara temporarily, and ultimately they are an undeceiving refuge that can place one in the ultimate, highest good.

Therefore, the great master [Padmasambhava] said:

The leaders of the world, no matter how excellent, are deceiving;
The sources of refuge, the three jewels, are undeceiving.

THE METHOD OF GOING FOR REFUGE

The way one should go for refuge is by having faith. The subcategories of faith are as follows.

Inspired faith: Faith arises temporarily through being inspired by the condition of seeing the life stories and positive qualities of noble beings, such as the three jewels.

Longing faith: By remembering the suffering of samsara, which is caused by the fault of unvirtuous actions, one develops the longing to be separated from it. Then, understanding the happiness of liberation into the higher realms due to the good qualities and benefits of virtue, one develops longing to obtain that.

Confident faith: Even when one is happy, one understands the kindness of the unsurpassable jewels. If one suffers, one understands it as the special blessing that purifies negative karma and so has confidence from the depths of one's heart.

Lord Atisha said:

The unsurpassable three jewels are the supreme refuge.
Rely well upon these objects of refuge
With the faiths of inspiration, longing, and confidence,
The excellent great fields of virtue.

Further, one goes for refuge in the Buddha as the teacher, in the dharma as the path, and in the sangha as the devoted companions who practice on the path.

THE COMMITMENTS TO PRACTICE

The commitments to practice are the conduct of what to abandon, what to adopt, and the conducive aspects.

What to Abandon

Having gone for refuge in the Buddha, do not seek refuge by putting your confidence in worldly gods, and do not prostrate to them. Having gone for refuge in the dharma, give up the thoughts and acts of harming life, such as beating and putting beings into bondage; rather, love them. Having gone for refuge in the sangha, do not spend time with negative people who do not have trust in karma and results or in the three jewels, whether they profess to be Buddhists or are actual non-Buddhist friends.

What to Adopt

Having gone for refuge in the Buddha, give up contempt or disrespect toward any representation of the Buddha, whether well formed or not. Perceive it as an object of respect just like the Buddha. Having gone for refuge in the dharma, abandon the karma of denigrating texts, down to a single letter, that have the Buddha's words, views, and explanations. With the thought that they are really the supreme jewel of the dharma, have respect. Having gone for refuge in the sangha, abandon contempt and discrimination toward those noble persons who uphold the pitakas and observe the vows; not only that, you should do so down to even unrighteous people who hold a mere sign of being a renunciate. Giving rise to the thought that they are the real sangha, have respect.

The Conducive Aspects

In thought and deed, always rely on the spiritual friend, the guru. Engage in hearing and contemplating the scriptures of the Victorious One and the words of the guru. Abandon the signs of worldliness—such as having contempt toward friends who act in accord with the dharma—and assume the signs of dharma. Further, however great the wealth you may encounter, do not abandon the three jewels. Whatever actions you may encounter, do not seek any other refuge. Always remember the qualities of the three jewels. You should diligently make offerings, and so forth; there are many such kinds of advice.

The *Letter to a Friend* states:

> In that way, even if a form of the Tathagata is made from wood,
> However it is made is suitable; wise ones make offerings to it.

The *Mind Ornament of Pleasant Sound* states:

> During the last five hundred years [of the age of my teaching],
> I will abide in the form of letters.
> Have the thought that they are me,
> And so at that time have respect for them.

The *Request of Adhyasaya Sutra* states:

> Conceit is the root of all heedlessness;
> Do not have contempt for even the lowliest monk.

Also, the Vinaya states:

> Even at the risk of your own life, or to gain an empire,
> Or even if just making a joke,
> Do not abandon the three jewels.

There are many such teachings.

THE BENEFITS OF GOING FOR REFUGE

Having been admitted as a Buddhist, you have become a receptacle for all the vows that keep one from being thrown into the lower realms. You will not be harmed by the obstacles of humans and nonhumans. You will have little illness and a long life. Previous karma and obscurations will be purified. Perfecting the cause, the two accumulations, you will quickly attain enlightenment.

To summarize, the *Condensed Prajnaparamita Sutra* states:

> If the merit of going for refuge were to take a form,
> The billionfold universe would be too small to contain it.

Accordingly, the benefits and qualities are inconceivable. Thus, the practice of going for refuge is the practice of the bodhisattvas.

8

LESSER BEINGS

The Sage taught that the sufferings of the lower realms,
Which are extremely difficult to bear, are the results of
   negative actions.
Therefore, even at the risk of one's own life,
To never commit negative actions is the practice of a
   bodhisattva. (8)

Fear arises through even hearing about the sufferings of the three lower realms. If their sufferings should actually come upon you, that experience, so very difficult to bear, will be unendurable.

It is not the case that the [experiences] of the lower realms with their torment are without causes or that they arise from causes that are not in accord with the result. Since the omniscient sages who had the attainment of wisdom taught that the lower realms are the result of the negative karma of the ten unvirtuous actions, do not ever engage in unvirtuous actions, even at the risk of your own life.

Furthermore, the path of lesser beings is (1) to contemplate suffering as the preliminary and, (2) out of fear of that, to distinguish causes and results and what to adopt and reject.

THE CONTEMPLATION OF SUFFERING

The *Precious Garland* states:

   Remind yourself daily
   Of the hells that are extremely hot and cold.

Also remember the hungry ghost realms
Where beings are emaciated due to hunger and thirst.
Remember the great many animals
With the sufferings of ignorance.

The Characteristics of the Eight Hot Hell Realms

With scorching iron as the ground, there are mountains, valleys, ravines, canyons, and carnivorous birds and beasts. There are many unruly guardians of hell who torture the beings there. The ebbing and flowing liquid of molten copper blazes fiercely. Tongues of fire of an arm's length constantly burn. Sharp spikes of iron form a sphere around the outer limits. Taking birth in this place that makes one tremble with fear is because of encountering unbearable cold in the bardo of becoming, like being swept away by a rainstorm: when one sees the abode of the hot hells and thinks that it is a warm place, then just like waking up from sleep, in that very instant one takes birth there.

The Particular Sufferings of the Various Hells

In the Rehealing Hell, the beings there pierce each other with weapons out of anger, and a rain of weapons falls from the sky, and so forth. There are many sufferings.

In the Black Line Hell, hell's guardians use a saw and a sword burning with fire to draw a line from the top of beings' heads to their toenails, cleave [each being in two], stick them back together, and then cleave them in two again.

In the Crushing Hell, there is a mountain of burning iron, the middle of which looks like the face of a sheep.[1] Like mustard seeds being turned into paste, beings there are ground; when their bodies become broken up, they are healed and then ground again.

In the Hell of Weeping and Wailing, if, out of agony, the beings look for a place to take shelter, they are put into a blazing house of iron, the door is closed, and they are scorched.

In the Hell of Great Weeping and Wailing, the sun [beats down] on an iron house with no doors, and fire gradually scorches those inside. One may escape through an inner door, but one will not be able to escape to the outside for a long time.

In the Hot Hell, the beings are scorched by a great fire burning inside a pot of iron or copper. On the ground of burning iron, their skin is peeled and stretched by stakes.

In the Very Hot Hell, in an iron pot with scalding boiling water, flesh rises to the rim, and the bones go to the bottom.

In the Hell of Endless Torment, beings' bodies are scorched like the wick of a butter lamp as they walk toward a great burning field. Only cries of torment are heard. One cannot distinguish the bodies from the flames, and they are ground into powder and so forth. There is no way to bear such sufferings. If one escapes, they are merely plunged into a pit where they are burned from four sides and cannot escape. If one escapes from that, they are submerged into mud made of rotten corpses. If one should escape from that, then on a mountain with a stake of iron one climbs up and down [chasing an object of desire] that one sees [but cannot obtain]. They are in great anguish. Escaping from that, being thirsty, the beings see a great river. If they come near it, they are plunged into a river of ashes and are tormented.

As for the life spans in these six hells, a single day in the hell realms from the Rehealing Hell to the Hot Hell is equal to the life span of the six types of desire gods, the four guardian kings, and so forth, which is equal to 120 million of our own years. The Very Hot Hell lasts half an aeon. In the Hell of Endless Torment one will remain for an entire aeon.

The Characteristics of the Different Types of Cold Hells

In the midst of darkness, nothing is apparent. In the middle of a great cliff of ice and snow, the beings there make shivering moans because of the wounds caused from the cold. This is called A Chu Chu.[2] In the Groaning Hell, there are cries of pain. In the Teeth-Chattering Hell, no cries come out.

[In the Blistering Hell], from coming in contact with the cold, the body is covered with blisters the size of one's big toe. Then the blisters burst and wounds appear.

In the Hell of Severe Cold, the body is broken into four pieces, like a lotus. The wounds that break open turn inside out, and the thin sinews, which are like a blue lotus (*utpala*), break into a thousand pieces. Breaking open like a great lotus, one is thrown into fragments. There is no way to bear the suffering.

As to the life span in the cold hells, the *Abhidharmakosha* states:

If, within a hundred bushels of sesame seeds, each seed is one
hundred years,
And one seed is pulled out every hundred years until they are all
exhausted,
That is the life span of a being in the Blistering Hell.
The life span in other cold hell beings is twenty times that.

From the Blistering Hell onward, each hell is twenty times as long [in life
span as the previous one]. They are realms where the suffering is difficult to
measure.
The Fifth Dalai Lama said:

In the house of burning iron, one is scorched by heat;
One is cut, dropped, and ground up, and a great river of blood pours
forth;
Rustling, blazing fire comes out of the orifices:
If this does not make you afraid, then a demon has entered your heart!

The Inconceivable Suffering of the Hungry Ghosts

The hungry ghosts with outer obscurations roam in every direction, pained
by hunger and thirst, but they do not find food or drink. Even if they see
it with their eyes, they are powerless to enjoy it because it is guarded by
the Lord of Death. When they see a fruit-bearing tree in a forest, the fruit
becomes a heap of charcoal. When they get near rivers, those also quickly
dry up. The climate too is reversed: in the summer months, the moon is
scorching, and in the winter, the sun is cool and causes unbearable cold, and
so forth. The sufferings are unbearable.

For those with inner obscurations, when they find a little bit of food and
drink, it changes into fire before it reaches their belly and burns, sears, and
scorches all their innards. Tongues of fire and smoke wind out from their
mouths, noses, and bellies.

The general obscurations are not being able to partake of food or drink
and having bodies that are in poor condition, weak, and have a blue-gray
color. Even if they find a little bit of food or drink, they cannot get any
through their mouths or throats because their mouths are only as big as the
eye of a needle, and their throats are as narrow as a hair from a horse's tail.

If something should reach their stomach, which is huge, like a vast land, it is never filled. The sufferings there are inconceivable.

The specific, personal obscurations refer to those hungry ghosts whose bodies have various particular defects. When they eat [they are not able to enjoy what they consume]. In addition to those, there are other indeterminate types of pleasure and pain.

As to their life span, the *Abhidharmakosha* states:

Each month is a day, and there are five hundred of those.

For every human month, there is one night, making their life span like five thousand of our own years.

The *Letter to a Friend* states:

After five thousand, even ten thousand years, their death does not come.

Their lives last five thousand years and sometimes, it is said, even ten thousand years.

Hungry ghosts that travel through the sky, such as *tsen, gyalpo, shin, dre, mamo*, and *theurang*,[3] act out only as frightening confused appearances. Every week, they must experience whatever harm previously caused their own death. Likewise, with the intention of sending their own suffering upon others, they harm beings, but it is of no benefit. The different types of oppression they must undergo—such as being overcome by the unbearable suffering caused by powerful *mantrikas'* activities of suppressing, scorching, and casting away—are incomprehensible.

The Fifth Dalai Lama said:

Now, in this short life, one works hard for the sake of food and
   drink.
[Compared to] eliminating the unbearable misery of hunger and
   thirst
Of fifty thousand human years,
Giving rise to the fortitude of letting go of this life is small.[4]

The Sufferings of Animals

Of the animals that live in hidden places, most live in the ocean. They live in places where the sun doesn't shine, where even if they stretch and fold their own limbs they can't see them. Here, bigger animals eat smaller ones, and smaller ones attack bigger ones. Every day, *naga*s are scorched by hot sand and are afraid of large birds of prey.

Animals that are scattered about, such as birds, cows, sheep, and other grazers and those that live in all the rivers, mountains, and four continents, also eat and harm one another. Humans kill them for the sake of their meat, skin, horns, and bones, without those animals having any power. Even if they are not able to bear them, they are encumbered with heavy loads. They are burdened with plowing, being milked, having their hair cut, being hit, being beaten, and so forth. In general, they endure the limitless sufferings of ignorance and stupidity.

The length of their life span is not definite. At the longest, some will experience suffering for an aeon.

As it is said:

> Since even the smallest pain from a wound is unbearable,
> The suffering of being killed for the sake of
> Their flesh, skin, and bones and being eaten is limitless.
> If that doesn't make your nerves shiver, then you're just a mindless
>   lug.

Merely hearing the enumerations of places in the lower realms makes one fearful. Should it actually befall you, the experience is extremely difficult to bear. Such are the torments of the lower realms.

The *Letter to a Friend* states:

> Writings about the hells, seeing or hearing about them,
> Remembering, reading about, or making an image of them
> Makes one suffer; what is there to say if you actually experience
> Such unbearable karmic results?

Having Fear of Suffering of the Lower Realms, the Classifications of Causes and Results, What to Adopt and Reject, and Examples of Those

The *Precious Garland* states:

> All suffering arises from nonvirtue.
> This applies accordingly to all beings of the lower realms.

Further, there are four general contemplations with respect to action and result: (1) the certainty of karma; (2) the vast quantity of karma; (3) not meeting with the result of actions that are not performed; and (4) no action committed goes to waste.

For contemplating actions and results in detail, the contemplations are the ten unvirtuous actions (the nonvirtues to be abandoned) and the opposite of those, the ten virtuous actions (the virtues that one should practice).

The Nonvirtues to Be Abandoned

There are three nonvirtues with respect to the body, such as killing; four with respect to speech— lying and so forth; and three with respect to mind, such as covetousness. For each of those, there are also three points: classifications, results, and particular cases.

Killing

There are three classifications of killing: Killing out of desire is killing in order to obtain wealth, meat, and skin. An example of killing out of anger is becoming competitive and spiteful and thus giving rise to anger and killing. Killing out of ignorance is killing with pretense toward virtue, such as taking the life of a non-Buddhist who does not know about virtue and nonvirtue or about cause and effect.

There are also three results of those: The fully ripened result is being born as a hell being. The result that is in accord with the cause is that, even if one is reborn as human, one's life will be short and one will have many sicknesses. The dominant result is being born in an inauspicious place.

In particular, among all the types of killing, killing one's parents and killing an arhat are extremely unvirtuous.

Taking What Is Not Offered

The three classifications: Stealing with force is forcefully taking from someone who is not at fault. An example of stealing through cunning is breaking into a house unnoticed and stealing. Stealing through deception is cheating someone by falsely measuring [goods].

The three results: The fully ripened result is taking birth as a hungry ghost. The result that is in accord with the cause is, even if one is born as a human, losing one's wealth and belongings. The dominant result is being born in a place where there is lots of hail.

In particular, among all the types of stealing, stealing the wealth of a guru or the supreme three jewels is extremely unvirtuous.

Sexual Misconduct Due to Desire

The three classifications: Sexual misconduct with those protected by class refers to engaging in sexual acts with relatives such as one's parents or siblings. Sexual misconduct with those who are protected by commitment refers to engaging in sexual acts with people who are in a relationship with another person. Sexual misconduct with those protected by dharma refers to such conduct with even your own spouse if it involves the wrong parts, such as the mouth and the anus;[5] the wrong place, such as a temple, stupa, or any one of many places of veneration; the wrong time, which is during *sojong*[6] or when a woman is pregnant or menstruating; or the wrong amount, which is more than five times in one night.

The three results: The fully ripened result is being born as a hungry ghost. The result that is in accord with the cause is becoming the youngest consort of a hostile enemy. The dominant result is being born in a place where there is dust and foul swamps.

In particular, among all the types of sexual misconduct, engaging in misconduct with one's mother or a female arhat is extremely unvirtuous.

Lying

The three classifications: Falsely claiming to be a guru means deceiving beings by saying that one has accomplished certain states that one has not accomplished. Great lies refers to telling lies that benefit oneself and harm others. Subtle lies means telling lies that do not harm or benefit anyone.

The three results: The fully ripened result is being born as an animal. The result that is in accord with the cause is being widely slandered. The dominant result is being born in a place that smells bad.

In particular, among all lies, slandering a buddha and lying to the guru are greatly unvirtuous.

Divisive Speech

The three classifications: Severe divisive speech means directly causing divisions in families and among dharma friends, masters, and disciples and creating factions within the sangha through one's speech. Indirect divisive speech means speaking indirectly about someone and causing friends to part from one another. Covert divisive speech means creating discord by speaking about someone indirectly and secretly with a malevolent intention and thus causing estrangement.

The three results: The fully ripened result is being born as a hell being. The result that is in accord with the cause is quickly having to part from friends once one has made them. The dominant result is being born in a place with extremes in high and low terrain.

In particular, instigating a schism between a teacher and student or within the sangha is greatly unvirtuous.

Harsh Speech

The three classifications: Direct harsh speech means speaking directly to others about their many kinds of faults. Indirect harsh speech means one indirectly criticizes another or, mixed with joking, one says many types of unkind things. Harsh speech by way of another means that through one's own coercion, another person speaks of someone's various faults.

The three results: The fully ripened result is being born as a hell being. The result that is in accord with the cause is that, even if born as a human, one will constantly hear all kinds of unpleasant words. The dominant result is being born in a land that is dry.

In particular, saying harmful words to a noble being or to one's parents is a great nonvirtue.

Useless Speech

The three classifications: Useless speech that turns from the right path means saying words and prayers conforming to non-Buddhist views. Worldly useless speech means speaking just for entertainment. Useless speech that rejects the truth refers to arguing against noble beings and teaching dharma to those who are not suitable vessels.

The three results: The fully ripened result is being born as an animal. The result that is in accord with the cause is that, even if born as a human, one does not have respectable speech and one is timid. The dominant result is being born in a place where summer and winter are reversed.

In particular, distracting a person who is practicing dharma is of great nonvirtue.

Covetousness

The three classifications: Covetousness with regard to oneself refers to great attachment to how one sees oneself, such as attachment to one's social class, wealth, beauty, and so forth. Covetousness of another's wealth means craving the accumulated possessions of another, having thoughts like, "How nice it would be if I could have that." Covetousness whose cause is neither oneself nor another refers to attachment to something such as gold, or a treasure that is under the earth; someone else does not own it, but one thinks, "How nice it would be to have that for myself."

The fully ripened result is being born as a hungry ghost. The result that is in accord with the cause is being born as someone who predominantly has desire, such as a prostitute. The dominant result is being born in a place where the grain is bad.

In particular, desiring to take away the belongings of dharma friends and noble beings is a great nonvirtue.

Maliciousness

The three classifications: Maliciousness that arises out of anger means wishing to do harm due to the arising of anger from fighting wars and so forth. Malicious mind that arises out of jealousy means being concerned about losing something to someone who is of higher status than oneself, rivals and so forth, and thinking about harming them. Maliciousness that arises out of resentment is, for example, when the malicious intention to kill arises because of resentment held toward someone's previous harm of them.

The fully ripened result is being born as a hell being. The result that is in accord with the cause is that others will not trust you and anger will be predominant. The dominant result is being born in a place where there is bitter and coarse food.

In particular, forming the intention to commit any of the five inexpiable deeds[7] is extremely unvirtuous.

Wrong Views

The three classifications: Having the wrong view of karma and result means not accepting that the results of virtue and nonvirtue are happiness and suffering, respectively. Having the wrong view of the four noble truths means maintaining that the truth of cessation, the result, cannot be accomplished through the truth of the path. Having the wrong view of the supreme jewels means not having faith in the three supreme ones and thus criticizing them.[8]

The fully ripened result of having wrong views is being born as an animal. The result that is in accord with the cause is predominantly having ignorance. And the dominant result is being born in a place where there are never any crops or harvest.

In particular, not having faith in the three jewels is greatly unvirtuous.

Each of these could also be explained according to distinctions in terms of mental afflictions, number, place, and so forth. If one did so, many elaborations could be made.

With regard to meritless karma, causes, and results, the *Precious Garland* says:

> Attachment, aggression, and ignorance—
> From the arising of these comes nonvirtue.
> From nonvirtue comes all suffering,
> And, likewise, so do all the lower realms.

The opposite of the ten nonvirtues are the ten virtues. The virtues of body are protecting the lives of others, giving generously, and engaging in sexual ethics. The virtues of speech are speaking honestly, bringing others together in close relationship, speaking peacefully and straightforwardly, and using meaningful speech. The virtues of mind are having little desire, having love and compassion, and relying on faith.

There are three results of these: The fully ripened result is being born in the human realm or the desire-god realm. The result that is in accord with the cause is not enjoying taking life; and thus because one saves lives, one's own life span will be long. The dominant result is being born in a place with wealth and great power.

With regard to actions and results of merit, the *Precious Garland* says:

> Having no attachment, anger, or ignorance—
> From the arising of these comes virtue.
> From virtue comes all beings' happiness, and
> Always giving rise to this, one accomplishes bliss.

Further, there are many kinds of nontransferring karma,[9] causes and results. Thus, if one contemplates the suffering of samsara, one will definitely give rise to compassion and so forth. If one contemplates actions and results, through trusting faith one will engage in what is to be adopted and rejected. This is the benefit of doing these contemplations. The opposite of that is the fault of not doing such contemplations.

The *Application of Mindfulness Sutra* says:

> Through virtue, happiness is obtained.
> From nonvirtue, suffering befalls you.
> Accordingly, the karma and results of
> Virtue and nonvirtue are clearly taught.

Lord Atisha also said:

> What is truly profound is none other than karma, [cause] and result. Obtaining stable trust in karma, cause and effect, is more supreme than seeing the face of the yidam deity.

Dromtönpa said:

> If one falls into the three lower realms,
> Because there is only suffering, there is not a single bit of happiness.

And:

> If you do not strive now for virtuous karma,
> It is certain you will experience suffering in the next life.

Potowa said:

> Having abandoned the ten nonvirtues, if we practice the ten virtues now, we will not find the three lower realms even if we look for them. Through abandoning the ten virtues and heedlessly engaging in the ten nonvirtues, we will not find the higher realms and liberation even if we look for them.

The Fifth Dalai Lama said:

> Formerly, by the power of nonvirtue, we were in the lower realms.
> Having experienced the unbearable suffering there, that was surely
>   enough!
> Now, you should establish perseverance well
> And accomplish the excellent body of the higher realms. Understand
>   this well!

In this way, having fear of the sufferings of the lower realms, bodhisattvas abandon and reject [the lower realms'] causes and results; this is the practice of the lesser being.

9

MIDDLING BEINGS

The pleasures of the three realms, like dewdrops on a blade
   of grass,
Are objects that perish in an instant.
To strive for the supreme state of liberation
That is never changing is the practice of a bodhisattva. (9)

In the three realms, or the three spheres of existence, whatever mundane happiness[1] you may find is like a drop of dew on a blade of grass. Since conditioned phenomena perish, [such happiness] lasts merely an instant, a single moment. Thus it is not suitable to be attached to it. Thus the supreme state of liberation that is never changing is perfect buddhahood; one should keep in mind at all times the special renunciation that strives toward that goal.

Further, the *Four Hundred Stanzas of Aryadeva* states:

To the wise ones, even the higher realms
Are like a hell realm, and so they give rise to fear.

If one considers the suffering of the three lower realms, which is so severe and difficult to bear, then one will understand that the three realms of samsara have only the slightest bit of mundane happiness within them. Further, since such happiness is without any essence, it is like a dewdrop on a blade of grass or like a flash of lightning. Phenomena last only a moment, which means, in reality, their nature is only suffering. In the same way, for every person in the realm of humans, big or small, there is a particular suffering befitting their size. In particular, all people have the suffering of birth, old age, sickness, and death; their wealth and riches decline; they come together and separate again; they are hit and beaten; they are killed, and so forth. The types of suffering are unfathomable. The jealous gods, due to the jealousy of being under others' power, always fight with each other; the suffering stemming from their fighting, such as defeat in war, is immeasurable.

The desire gods[2] also, through heedlessness and being intoxicated with desire, have the suffering of change and falling at the time of their death. They must experience suffering that is like a fish floundering in hot sand for seven days of the god realm. In the two higher realms, even though they are not afflicted by strong suffering for some time, they have the suffering of change. Just as a bird that flies in the sky must fall to the ground, they are plunged again to the lower realms because the power of their contaminated virtue[3] has been exhausted. They must experience severe suffering. Further, all of them have all-pervasive suffering, which is just like eating poisonous food or fighting against the skill of a powerful wrestler.[4] Through grasping on to conditioned composite things, you will never go beyond being without freedom.

The sutras say:

> In samsara, there is not even
> A needle point's worth of happiness.

Maitreya said:

> Just as waste is without a pleasant odor,
> The five types of beings do not have happiness.[5]

The spiritual friend Jamyang Gawa said:

> At this time, when we have well obtained the support of a human
>   birth with the freedoms and resources
> And understand the main points of the three trainings,
> If we don't defeat the army of the source of all suffering,
> We will have to endure again the weary plain of birth and death.

Accordingly, that all of samsara is the source of suffering is the truth of suffering. If we understand this, we will develop our striving toward liberation and due to that, attain nirvana.

The *Udanavarga* states:

If we realize these faults,
We will quickly attain nirvana.

All the suffering of samsara arises due to its origin, karma. Karma, in turn, arises due to its origin, the mental afflictions. This is the truth of the origin [of suffering].

The root of all these mental afflictions is self-clinging, and the opposite of that—the cessation that is the pacification of suffering, or the ability to realize liberation—is called the truth of cessation.[6] This liberation means being liberated from the bonds of karma and mental afflictions. The path that liberates is the practice of the three trainings. Among the three trainings, actually turning from self-fixation, which is the root of samsara, is the training in the prajna that realizes selflessness. This depends on samadhi and the root of all of its good qualities, discipline. This is the truth of the path.

Actualizing the four noble truths turns this body we have now from rebirth. One should train by striving in the activity that attains liberation free from rebirth.

The Second Buddha, Padmakara, said:

Should one strive for worldly deeds, there will be no end;
If you will strive in the dharma, you should act quickly.
Even the good deeds of samsara will, in the end, decline,
Yet the results of the conduct of genuine dharma will never
    diminish.
From beginningless time, having habituated and continually
    engaged
In karma, mental afflictions, and habitual tendencies, we have
    accumulated karma unceasingly.
Due to that, we have deluded perceptions and wander in samsara.
At this time, we do not pay heed to liberation.
Even if you remember at the time of death, it is far too late.
Just as medicine will not be of help if one's head is cut off,
For that reason, thoroughly understanding all the sufferings of
    samsara,
Place yourself perfectly in the abode of peace.

Lord Atisha said:

Friends, this swamp of samsara is without happiness; go to the dry land of liberation.

And also:

Even if you observe the three vows, if you do not have revulsion toward samsara, then they become the cause for samsara.

Similarly, Zilnön Draktsal said:

Just as a bird flying in the expanse of sky
In the end must fall back to the earth,
Even after going to the peak of existence, by circling like a firebrand
In these three realms, you will be disheartened.

Thus, bodhisattvas, not being attached to samsara's happiness, strive for the sake of liberation. This is the practice of the middling being.

GIVING RISE TO THE SUPREME INTENTION
OF BODHICHITTA

From beginningless time, my mothers have loved me.
If they suffer, how can I worry about my own happiness?
Therefore, in order to liberate sentient beings, which are
    boundless,
To engender bodhichitta is the practice of a bodhisattva. (10)

In samsara without beginning, our kind mothers who gave us birth, the
sentient beings of the six realms, have cherished us more than their own
lives, with great immeasurable love. Yet we do not give any thought to their
torment, their drawn-out suffering in the lower realms and samsara. How
can we strive only for the sake of the happiness of the higher realms, or even
for the peace of the solitary realizers and hearers, just for ourselves?

Therefore, just as the previous buddhas gave rise to bodhichitta in order
to attain buddhahood to liberate all sentient beings without limit from
samsara, likewise, thinking, "I too must engender supreme bodhichitta,"
precede that with loving-kindness and compassion.

Further, the *Ornament of Clear Realization* states:

Engendering bodhichitta is the desire to attain
Complete, perfect enlightenment in order to benefit beings.

Giving rise to bodhichitta with the aspiration or the intention of benefiting
others has seven points: (1) the root, understanding sentient beings to be

your mother; (2) remembering their kindness; (3) repaying that kindness; (4) loving-kindness; (5) compassion; (6) joy; and (7) equanimity.

THE ROOT, UNDERSTANDING ALL SENTIENT BEINGS TO BE YOUR MOTHER

Wherever space pervades, so do sentient beings; and wherever sentient beings pervade, so are there those whose nature is only suffering. Since the beginningless time of samsara until now, there is not a single one of these beings who has not been our parent, and the number of times they have been our parents is countless.

The *Letter to a Friend* states:

> If all mother sentient beings whom we have met were merely the size
>   of a juniper berry,
> Even the whole earth could not hold their number.

REMEMBERING THEIR KINDNESS

How much kindness has our mother shown us? There was the kindness of giving birth to us, the kindness of undergoing hardship for our sake, the kindness of giving us life, the kindness of teaching us the ways of the world, and so forth. It is unfathomable.

The *[Prajnaparamita Sutra in] Eight Thousand Verses* states:

> Why? Our mother gave birth to us and did it with joy. She gave
> us our life and taught us the ways of the world.

The pain our mothers endured while caring for us with their immeasurable love is unfathomable. We do not understand the kindness of our mothers who cared for us with inconceivable benefit. Not thinking of this at all and seeking out peace and happiness for our own benefit is utterly shameless. For great beings, it is a disgrace. It is the worst deviation on the Mahayana path.

REPAYING THEIR KINDNESS

For the reason stated above, in order to attain buddhahood to liberate all sentient beings, equal to the limits of space, from the great suffering of samsara, the bodhisattvas of the past practiced for the benefit of others. Thus, we should also cultivate the wish to practice accordingly.

The *Entrance to the Way of a Bodhisattva* states:

> Just as the previous buddhas
> Have given rise to the heart of enlightenment . . .

And:

> Likewise, gradually, in those trainings
> I will abide and train myself.[1]

IMMEASURABLE LOVING-KINDNESS

All sentient beings are like the analogy of a small child who is ungrateful toward their parents' care. [Even though parents] disregard all of their own hardships, the child strives with body, speech, and mind only toward ways to make themselves comfortable and happy and to make things easy for themselves. Similarly, sentient beings wish for happiness, but even though they desire it, they are not skillful in achieving it. They do not understand that engaging in virtue is the cause of happiness. Committing the ten unvirtuous actions, they are mistaken in their wishes and actions, and so sentient beings have only suffering. In accord with each and every one of their individual desires, meditate again and again, thinking, "How wonderful it would be for them to have only peace and happiness."

The *Entrance to the Way of a Bodhisattva* says:

> When you look upon sentient beings,
> Look at them straightforwardly and with loving-kindness.[2]

Even if you only look upon other sentient beings [and do not try to create any tangible benefit], look upon them gently with a smile. In short, whatever you do, it should be done only with loving-kindness. It is said that boundless loving-kindness[3] is like a mother hen caring for her chicks. When she cares for them, first she makes a soft, comfortable nest. Then, with her wing she shelters them close to her and keeps them warm. Until the chicks are able to fly, she cares for them with gentleness in all that she does. Just like that, you should practice loving-kindness toward all beings of the three realms with your body, speech, and mind.

IMMEASURABLE COMPASSION

Wherever space pervades, there pervade sentient beings. And wherever sentient beings pervade, so does there pervade negative karma and suffering. The ones who experience such suffering and negative karma have all been our parents throughout our lifetimes. Now, in this abode of suffering—the three realms of samsara—beings must continuously experience its nature of *dukkha*,[4] so difficult to bear. When we think, "How sad!" for our tormented parents—these deluded ones—something unbearable arises in our hearts.

Giving rise to such compassion is said to be like the child of an armless mother being carried away by a river. If the child of a mother with no arms is being carried away by a river, the mother gives rise to the unbearable suffering of love and compassion toward her child. But because she has no arms, the mother is unable to pull the child out of the water. With the thought, "What can I do?" she thinks only of a way to help. She lets out a cry of devastation and runs. Like that, the river of suffering carries away all sentient beings of the three realms. Cultivate unbearable compassion for those who are drowning in the ocean of samsara.

Potowa said:

> For example: A poisonous snake that shoots his poison into the sky hits birds in flight, both large and small. Because of the poison, the birds let out a cry of agony without any control. All of them fall into the mouth of the snake. Likewise, when those who have compassion see the suffering of sentient beings, unable to bear it, they will uncontrollably act for others' benefit.

In this way, immeasurable compassion is indispensable. The sutras say:

> Wherever there is a head, there is life.
> Wherever there is compassion, there is bodhichitta.
> Wherever there is bodhichitta, there is buddhahood.

IMMEASURABLE JOY

Immeasurable joy is having joy over the permanent liberation of all sentient beings, equal to space, from their current state of not going beyond the nature of suffering. [In particular, one should aspire that beings may] quickly attain the level of buddhahood that is perfect bliss and, temporarily, that they be placed on the level of the higher realms of the gods and humans. Through the power of their own karma, some sentient beings have good qualities, wealth, and power. Even if they obtain only the slightest bit of these, without becoming jealous or competitive, cultivate the thought that through this they may be even further enriched by many perfections such as great wisdom, nonharm, and the wealth of the glorious higher realms. Meditate thinking, "How happy I would be if other beings also dwelled in such a state."

Thus, completely draw out, by the root, the negative mind that cannot bear others' wealth and accumulations. You should give rise to joy toward all aspects of happiness. If your mind stream is not so, then, tainted by jealousy, thereafter you will accrue the grave nonvirtue of not recognizing the qualities of others.

Long ago, Darlo, a teacher of debate, was a jealous adversary of Milarepa. Due to that, he was later born as a great demon. For those who have such jealousy, even if a real buddha comes, that buddha will not have the power to guide them. Tainted by jealousy in their mind stream, they do not consider the qualities of a buddha. Because of not considering those qualities, they do not give rise to faith. Not giving rise to faith, they are not suitable vessels.

Devadatta and Sunakshatra, with their minds of jealousy and competitiveness toward the Buddha, did not wish to generate even a little bit of faith. Although they were in the presence of the Buddha in their own lifetime, there was no way to tame them.

If you have merely the negative attitudes of competitiveness and jealousy, it will not harm others at all. However, you will pointlessly accumulate strong negativity for yourself. Thus abandon such negative attitudes. At all times, meditate from the depths of your heart on joy in others' wealth and qualities.

Such immeasurable joy is said to be like a camel finding its lost calf. Camels, compared to other sentient beings, have surpassing love for their young. For a mother camel who is deeply tormented merely by the loss of her calf, inconceivable joy will arise in her should she find him. Train in accord with this example.

IMMEASURABLE EQUANIMITY

In the same way, you should train in equanimity toward all sentient beings—not having attachment or aggression toward those who are close or distant. Right now, as we are going unchecked, we are strongly attached to our parents, relatives, and so forth. Our untamed aggression toward our enemies and our dislike for their circle of acquaintances has the fault of a complete lack of scrutiny. The enemies we have now were, in previous lifetimes, close to us and kept our company with love, and because of that friendship, they cared for us. The benefit they gave us is unfathomable. Also, the friends we have now were our enemies in previous lives and indeed also did many harmful things to us.

Arya Katyana said:

> The father becomes meat to eat and the mother gets beaten;
> Bad karmic enemies are kept in one's lap;
> One spouse gnaws on the bones of the other:
> The phenomena of samsara make me laugh.

The loving concern that we have for our current parents and for the relatives with whom we have a connection is inconceivable. We do not wish for harm to come to them. Should it occur, our pain is even greater than if it happened to us; however, previously, we mutually repaid each other's harm.

The enemies we have now were, without a doubt, our parents in other lives. Now too, it is uncertain whether they will do harm to us. Those whom we hold as our enemies may not consider us to be their enemy. Those who do consider us their enemy may not be able to harm us. Also, whatever may harm us in this moment may turn out to be a support for bringing us happiness, such as causing us to meet the dharma and thus bringing us ultimate benefit and happiness. Likewise, there are also those whom we regard as close now [but might not be in the future], such as a child who betrays their parents and does them harm. Should that happen, then by taking those who appear for the moment as friends or enemies to be real, you will accumulate the negative karma of attachment and aggression and bring about the sinking rock of the lower realms. What is the use of that?

Nagarjuna [in *Letter to a Friend*] says:

> The father becomes the son and the mother becomes the wife.
> Once they were enemies; now they are friends.

Things get turned around, and that is why
There is not a bit of certainty in samsara.

Thoroughly establish in your mind the thought that all sentient beings equal to the limits of space were your parents, and you their child. Have the view of friends and enemies as being equal.

If you do that, you will have immeasurable equanimity that is said to be like a sage throwing a banquet. When a sage throws a banquet for guests, he throws it for everyone, without any regard for high or low class, relative or unrelated, good or bad. You should have equanimity toward the objects of compassion, which are all sentient beings who pervade all of space. Until you are able to do that, train your mind.

Lord Atisha said:

Love and compassion are to be cultivated,
And bodhichitta is to be made stable.

And:

Bodhichitta that is connected with
Great compassion is praised as supreme.

Dromtönpa said:

Loving-kindness, compassion, and bodhichitta are the cause for accomplishing great benefit for both oneself and others.

Rinchen Gang said:

Without the mind of altruism,
The vows of aspiration and application bodhichitta will not arise
And there will be no mastery of the Mahayana dharma;
Thus, loving-kindness and compassion are very important.

Thus, giving rise to bodhichitta preceded by loving-kindness and compassion is the bodhisattva practice of giving rise to bodhichitta.

11
MEDITATION OF EXCHANGING SELF
AND OTHERS

All suffering, without exception, arises from the desire for
  one's own happiness.
Perfect buddhas are born from benefiting others.
Therefore, to perfectly exchange one's own happiness
For others' suffering is the practice of a bodhisattva. (11)

In this realm of samsara, all of the suffering there is, without exception,
arises from self-cherishing due to wishing for one's own happiness. Whatever mundane or transcendent happiness and benefit there is—such as the
ultimate happiness on the level of a perfect buddha—all of it is born from
the intention to benefit and cherish others. Therefore, whatever happiness
and virtue you may have, send it to sentient beings. And whatever suffering
and negativity beings have, take it on for yourself. In this way, exchange
happiness and suffering.

 Also, the *Entrance to the Way of a Bodhisattva* states:

Whatever happiness there is in the world,
It all comes from the desire for others' happiness.
Whatever suffering there is in the world,
It all comes from the desire for happiness for oneself.
What need is there to say any more?
We immature ones do things for ourselves,
And the buddhas work for the benefit of others.
Consider the difference between these two![1]

THE FAULTS OF CHERISHING ONESELF

In this realm of samsara, no matter how much suffering one has, every bit of it, without any left out, comes from cherishing oneself. In samsara, nothing ever goes the way one wishes it to. The coming together of friends and loved ones hoping for happiness through love and affection toward each other is a conditioned phenomenon; they will be parted without any control. In most cases, someone will die. Or, should misfortune come upon them due to enemies and harmful events that scatter them in different directions, that suffering is inconceivable.

Further, hoping for happiness, someone builds a house, [but then, collapsing,] it kills them. Hoping to have their hunger satisfied, someone eats food, but then the food causes a life-threatening illness. Desiring to make some profit, you engage in business, and enemies defeat you and you become poor; the list could go on. All of this life's striving in the hopes of attaining happiness and wealth is only the cause of suffering.

Omniscient Longchenpa said:

Though we desire to always be near our relatives and loved ones,
It is certain we will part.
Though we desire to always remain in this comfortable home,
It is certain we will leave it.
Though we desire never to be separated from the enjoyment of this
    wealth and happiness,
It is certain it will be left behind.

However great the wealth we have, that is how great our suffering will be. Because we are never satisfied, we accrue it and protect it. During the day we work to make our wealth grow, and at night we guard it. We pass the time always and only for the sake of maintaining it.

Nagarjuna said:

Accruing, protecting, and proliferating are exhausting:
Know that wealth brings boundless ruin.

Panchen Chögyen said:

Self-cherishing is the gateway to all decline.

All suffering comes from taking there to be a self where there is no self and taking there to be an "I" where there is no "I." All of this dukkha of karma and mental afflictions, whose nature is so difficult to bear, comes from the fault of clinging to a self.

THE BENEFITS OF CHERISHING OTHERS

Bodhichitta, the exchange of self and other, is the unerring, ultimate essence. It is the object of meditation of all who engage the path of the Mahayana dharma. Even from arising in one's mind stream once, it will perfect vast accumulations of merit and wisdom and will clear away the obscurations and nonvirtue of many aeons. It liberates one from the lower realms and from birthplaces that plunge one back into the lower realms. The benefits are inconceivable.

It is said that, long ago, the first time the Buddha of our time benefited others, he was born as a charioteer in the hell realms,[2] and then as a daughter of a friend, and so forth.[3] This can be understood from numerous such stories.

Lord Atisha said:

Because of the negative result of the faults of attachment and confusion,
Habituate the mind to exchanging self and other.

Langthangpa said:

Even by opening up just a bit of the profound dharma and looking into it, [I see that] all faults are my own; all of the qualities are those of noble sentient beings. The key point is this: May profit and victory be given to others, and may loss and defeat be taken on myself. It shouldn't be understood to be anything but this.

The Fifth Dalai Lama said:

When the mind of self-cherishing is given up,
With the key of repaying harm with benefit,
The gate of welfare that spontaneously accomplishes the two benefits
Is immediately opened. How wondrous is this great fortune!

Perfectly exchanging the mind of cherishing oneself with the mind of giving to others is the bodhisattva practice of meditating on exchanging self and other.

12

TAKING TO THE PATH NOT GETTING WHAT YOU WANT

Even if someone, out of intense desire, steals all my wealth
Or makes another do so,
To dedicate my body, possessions, and all virtue of the three
   times
To them is the practice of a bodhisattva. (12)

Should sentient beings, whoever they may be, through the force of intense craving and desire, steal all of your wealth and possessions, or if they make someone else steal them, do not take revenge on them out of anger. Not only that, with the intention of benefiting them, dedicate and offer your body, your possessions, and whatever virtue you have accumulated in the three times, again and again, to the one who does you harm.

Also, the *Entrance to the Way of a Bodhisattva* states:

These possessions of mine I will abandon,
But my negativity will firmly remain with me.[1]

Since honor and gain are the source of many faults, it is irrational to be happy about obtaining them. You should understand that honor and gain are a hindrance. Your wealth being stolen will naturally release your mind from its clinging. It is like the gateway of not being sent to the lower realms. By giving up your body, possessions, roots of virtue, and so forth, repay their kindness.

Lord Atisha said:

Do not get angry with those who harm you. However much you do become angry at the one who harms you, that much you must practice patience.

And:

Honor and gain are objects of abandonment.
Pride is always to be given up.

Chen-ngawa said:

For example, if you do not set up a target, an arrow will not hit it. Placing the target is the root condition for it being hit by the arrow. Likewise, due to our placing the target of our previous bad karma, others shoot the arrow of harm toward us in this life. Therefore, it is said that one should not become angry with others.

In that way, abandon becoming prideful over obtaining honor and wealth, and abandon having a negative intention toward those who do you harm. Training solely in the wish to be of benefit is the bodhisattva practice of taking loss to the path.

13

TAKING SUFFERING TO THE PATH

Should someone sever my head
Even though I did not do the slightest wrong,
Through the power of compassion, to take on
Their negativity for myself is the practice of a bodhisattva. (13)

Without your having done even the slightest wrong, such as harming another, should someone cut off your arms, legs, and so forth—or not only that, should they sever the most important part, your head—whatever they may do, do not engage in the negative intention or conduct of returning such harm to them out of anger. Through the condition of engaging in such great nonvirtue, you will experience suffering. Therefore, with a mind of compassion toward them, take on for yourself their negativity and their resultant suffering.

Also, the *Entrance to the Way of a Bodhisattva* states:

When overpowered by the mental afflictions,
Some even kill their own cherished self.
If that is so, how could it not be
That the afflictions harm others.[1]

For example, should a crazy person harm another, if those nearby are of sound mind, none of them will condemn that person. Accordingly, the demon of strong mental afflictions is a great, possessed madman that harms us. Meditate on loving-kindness and compassion toward their suffering. It is irrational to become angry.

Also, if harm should come upon your body, you should understand that it is the weapon of the negative karma of your previously having done harm to someone else.

Lord Atisha said:

> When harm befalls your body,
> View it as your previous karma.

Not only that, the great beings of the past practiced the commitment of repaying all harm done to them only with benefit. Once, the lord of dharma Götsangpa was robbed and all of his provisions were stolen. His body was wickedly beaten and tormented in many other ways. Later, the thief was put into prison at Ralungse. Götsangpa went there and, seeing the thief, said to the attendant, "That man has done great kindness to me. Put me in prison in place of him," and so the thief was released from prison.

Similarly, the great being Ngulchu Tokmé, in the story of removing lice from the louse-ridden man, is particularly noble.[2] In this way, you should understand the good qualities of not being disheartened by any harm or suffering.

Sharawa said:

> You should understand that harm and suffering are conditions
> for the dharma.

Langthangpa said:

> When you see beings that have a malicious nature
> Or are overwhelmed by suffering and nonvirtue,
> As if you had encountered a precious treasure
> That is difficult to find, cherish them.

Thus, whatever suffering befalls you, such as undeserved harm done by others, do not repay that harm. Moreover, to understand that they will experience suffering through the condition of their intense negativity and, by the power of the compassion that wishes them to be free from such suffering and nonvirtue, to take on for oneself their negativity and its result—the suffering [that will ripen]—is the bodhisattva practice of taking suffering onto the path.

14

TAKING BLAME TO THE PATH

Even if some should proclaim unpleasant things
About me throughout the three-thousand-fold universe,
With a mind of loving-kindness, to speak of their good
    qualities
In return is the practice of a bodhisattva. (14)

Even if some others broadcast throughout the three-thousand-fold universe various unpleasant things secretly blaming you, do not harm them by saying unpleasant things in return out of anger and so forth. Not only that, with a mind of loving-kindness that wishes for happiness and joy to arise in the mind of that harm doer, proclaim their good qualities in return.

    Also, the *Entrance to the Way of a Bodhisattva* says:

If you say you are angry at others' unpleasant speech toward you
Because they are doing damage to others,
Why do you not get angry
When they say such unpleasant things to others?[1]

The bodhisattvas do not ever get angry about unpleasant things said. Not only that, whatever disrespect or slander they may encounter, they never become angry. In particular, the blame we receive now is said to be the weapon of the previous karma of our own coarse speech.

    The *Precious Garland* says:

Because of coarse speech, blame is heard.

Regarding the bodhisattvas, such as the previous Kadampa masters, there are only stories telling of them never having the slightest anger toward ingratitude shown by others.

Lord Atisha said:

> When one hears unpleasant words,
> Regard them as echoes.

Langthangpa also said:

> Train in taking on defeat that is undeserved—
> Such as abuse and denigration
> Due to others' jealousy toward us—
> And sending victory to others.

In that way—not holding those who say unpleasant things at fault and not getting angry—speaking of the qualities of others and not speaking of their faults is the bodhisattva practice of taking blame to the path.

15

TAKING DENIGRATION TO THE PATH

Even if several people in the midst of a crowd
Should reveal my hidden faults and speak harsh words,
To hold them to be my spiritual friends
And bow to them with respect is the practice of a
bodhisattva. (15)

In the midst of a gathering of many people, even if several people say very coarse, harsh words that are abusive or that reveal your hidden faults—such as, "In regard to spiritual and worldly life, he has such and such faults"—abandon your anger and do not repay that harm. Not only that, because of the great kindness of their showing your hidden faults, you should bow down with the same respect you have toward your spiritual friend.

Also, the *Entrance to the Way of a Bodhisattva* says:

If there are others who blame me,
Why should I be happy when I am praised?
And if there will be others who praise me,
Why should I be unhappy when blamed?[1]

It is irrational to have attachment, anger, like, or dislike toward praise and denigration. In particular, even if something intolerable happens, like someone denigrating you or revealing your faults, take that person to be a supreme master who is giving you oral instructions and repay their kindness with respect.

Lord Atisha said:

The supreme spiritual friend is the one who confronts your faults.
The supreme oral instruction is that which strikes at those faults.

Langthangpa also said:

If someone whom I've benefited
In hopes of benefit in return
Should do me some undeserved harm,
I will train in the view of their being a genuine spiritual friend.

Accordingly, should people gather around you, scowling, whatever insults they say that point out your hidden faults, immediately think that such words, endowed with love, are cutting your faults—the poison tree of pride—from the root, and because of that are very kind. This is the relative view. As for the absolute view, the *Entrance to the Way of a Bodhisattva* says:

As things, in this way, are empty,
What is there to gain? What is there to lose?[2]

From the ultimate point of view, all utterances—whether of praise or of blame (including the pointing out of hidden faults, disgrace, or degeneration) —are devoid of anything to gain or to lose. Knowing them to have the essence of sound-emptiness, and so forth, is the way bodhisattvas carry denigration to the path.

16

TAKING INGRATITUDE TO THE PATH

Even if someone I cared for like my child
Should act as though I were their enemy,
Like a mother toward her child stricken with illness,
To love them even more is the practice of a bodhisattva. (16)

Even if someone whom you cared for—always cherishing them as your own
child, with spiritual and material support—has harmed you with their three
gates and acts as though you were their enemy, do not return such harm
out of anger. Moreover, if an insane child who is stricken with illness and
malevolent spirits commits various acts of harm toward their mother, the
mother does not hold a grudge against them. With love, she thinks, "May
my child be free of such sickness." Just so, with the thought, "This one who
has harmed me has done wrong because of having come under the power of
the mental afflictions; how wonderful it would be if they were free of such
mental afflictions," you should, with even more love, give rise to benefiting
them in thought and deed.

Also, the *Ornament of the Sutras* states:

Those beings who, without any control, are always at fault—
The bodhisattvas, being wise, do not regard them as blameworthy.
They say, "Against their own will, they turn from [what will make
them happy],"
And their compassion increases toward those beings.

Accordingly, even though immature ones who become powerless due to the
power of the mental afflictions do ungrateful things, the wise bodhisattvas

do not hold them to be blameworthy in any way. Their love and compassion expand toward such beings. Thus, not giving rise to loving-kindness and compassion toward those with negative dispositions and great nonvirtue, and who return benefit with harm, is a sign of the student not being trained. Chekhawa said:

> Though one may repay your benefit with harm,
> Meditate on repaying that, in turn, with great compassion.

Whatever ungratefulness is repaid to your kindness, know that this is the way of immature ones who are under the control of the mental afflictions. You should show them even more love. This is the way bodhisattvas bring the ungratefulness of others onto the path.

17

TAKING OTHERS' CONTEMPT TO THE PATH

Even if someone my equal or lower
Should insult me influenced by pride,
To place them with respect, as if they were a guru,
At the crown of my head is the practice of a bodhisattva. (17)

If someone who is equal to you in class, looks, wealth, and so forth, or if
those who are lower than you should, influenced by pride, belittle or insult
you in various ways, do not get angry with them. Rather, with your three
gates, bow down with respect as if they were your guru endowed with great
kindness. You should place them at the crown of your head.

Also, the *Entrance to the Way of a Bodhisattva* states:

Should many people trample, beat, or even kill me,
I will not rise up against them. Now, protectors of the world, rejoice!

And:

Likewise, should someone weak do the slightest harm to me,
I should not belittle them.[1]

Even if someone does you harm, whether they are of high or low status, you
should regard them as a buddha and show them respect. It is improper to
have contempt or look down upon one who harms you. Should you return
such harm, that person's anger will increase markedly and your own virtuous conduct will decrease. Because of that, both of you will become imbued
with faults. One who doesn't return such harm will become a great faultless

being endowed with patience. Therefore, among all those with patience toward harm done to them, those who are especially humble are truly wondrous. Further, you should regard sentient beings as gurus, wish-fulfilling jewels, and so forth.

Nagarjuna said:

> The cause, the phenomenon that is concordant
> With enlightenment, is sentient beings;
> Thus, with the desire for perfect enlightenment,
> Regard sentient beings as the guru.

Chen-ngawa said:

> Worldly beings regard buddhas more dearly than sentient beings.
> We should do the opposite: Buddhists should cherish sentient
> beings.

As to the reason for that: it is not that one should not have respect for the buddhas; however, since sentient beings have been our parents, we should see them as our mothers, remember their kindness, repay that kindness, and care for them. Not only that, through the many key points of dharma, such as "Sentient beings are the only cause for buddhahood," one should understand the reason it is necessary to cherish sentient beings.

Contrary to that, if you think, "I will do harm to someone who has done harm to me," and "I will never do them benefit," should a single period[2] go by when you do not apply the antidote, you will have the fault of abandoning sentient beings. Not only that, you will have committed the root downfall of casting away bodhichitta. Having the intention of repaying harm with benefit is included in most of the mind trainings and samayas. This is the bodhisattva practice of bringing contempt to the path.

18

Taking Loss to the Path

Even when I am made destitute, people constantly berate
me,
And grave illness and evil spirits strike me,
To take on still the suffering and misdeeds of all beings for
myself
Without losing heart is the practice of a bodhisattva. (18)

Whether you are without wealth and possessions to start with or enemies
have stolen what you previously had, if you become destitute[1] and poor,
with even the food you need for sustenance declining; or, furthermore, if
people constantly berate you and condescend you; and, on top of that, you
are stricken by grave illness such as leprosy and evil spirits such those that
reside above,[2] causing you to suffer immensely—in spite of all this, considering the torment of your own suffering, through the strength of compassion,
think, "I will forbear whatever torment from suffering others have." Take
for yourself all of the suffering of every sentient being. Regarding whatever
poverty, illness, or evil spirits you may encounter, reflect on patience, without the slightest bit of apprehension or loss of heart. You should do this with
determination.

Also, the *Precious Garland* says:

Even if degenerate like a hungry ghost,
Do not become disheartened.

Whatever suffering or undesirable situation you encounter, you should not
become discouraged; rather, give rise to courage and take it to the path. If

you understand that, faults will arise as good qualities, suffering will arise as happiness, and obstacles and hindrances to dharma will not harm you. Potowa said:

> Among businessmen [in Tibet], it is said that snow in the mountains benefits their horses' hooves, and enemies do not come when rain falls at night.[3] As in those analogies, bringing sickness, poverty, slander, and even the suffering of a dream to the path has many good qualities such as purifying negativities.

Kharakpa said:

> Through even the slightest suffering we experience now,
> We are exhausting the suffering caused by previous deeds.
> In the next life, it will become happiness.
> Meditate, joyfully, on suffering!

And:

> Adverse conditions are a spiritual friend.
> Obstacles are what urge one to spiritual practice.
> Suffering is the broom that sweeps away negativity.
> Do not see an unhappy mind as unfortunate!

The lord of dharma Götsangpa said:

> The dharma is opened through adverse conditions.

Even though [Ngulchu Tokmé] carried on him a quart of lice for a long time, because he took it to the path, whatever suffering he had didn't make him disheartened.
 Shantideva said:

> Without suffering, there is no renunciation;
> Misery dispels pride.
> Give rise to compassion for samsaric beings;
> Shun negativity and delight in virtue.

It is said that suffering is the cause for leading one to many qualities.
Patrul Orgyen Jikme Chökyi Wangpo said:

Do not delight in happiness, delight in suffering.
With happiness, the five poisons—the afflictions—will grow.
With suffering, previously accumulated bad karma is exhausted.
Suffering is the compassion of the guru.

Suffering is the master that teaches the faults of samsara; it is the direct
cause for the practice of compassion and patience; it is the delineation point
of dharma; it is the condition for purifying obscurations; it has unfathomable [such good qualities]. That the previous masters viewed suffering as an
ornament is written of many times in their life stories.
Serling Chökyi Drakpa said:

Ghosts and evil spirits are emanations of the victorious ones.
Adverse conditions are spiritual friends.
Sickness is what sweeps away negativities and obscurations.
Suffering is the shifting mist of dharmata.[4]
To tame the people of the hinterlands,
These four points must be abandoned, adopted, engaged, and
collected [respectively].
You should have patience in this age of degeneration
Toward negative karma that comes back to you.

This has been said many times. Not only that:
Panchen Chögyen said:

The world and its contents are completely filled with the results of
nonvirtue.
Although the suffering of not getting what we want falls like rain,
Grant your blessings that we may take negative conditions to the path
And see them as the cause for the exhaustion of negative karma's
results.

The results of our ten negative actions in this world, which is the vessel, are
extremely rampant. Sentient beings, its contents, do not exist apart from

what is produced by the mind—the mental afflictions—and what is produced by actions, the accumulation of negative karma. By the force of that, the power of evil ones spreads, and thus in general, the practice of dharma is diminished far and wide. In particular, at this time when those who practice the Mahayana struggle with [adverse] conditions, if one does not put the dharma into practice by bringing them to the path, it will be extremely difficult to perfect the dharma. When this is put into practice, adverse conditions will be subsumed into harmonious conditions. All obstacles will appear as friends.

If you consider all harmful deeds to be the guru who is encouraging you toward the dharma, and if you know how to carry this to the path, all negative conditions will appear as aids that help you to accomplish enlightenment.

As to these oral instructions of taking adverse conditions to the path, there were many noble ones who came before amid the snow mountains [of Tibet] and did many praiseworthy deeds that were especially profound, such as taking the instructions of equal taste to the path. May those who truly wish to practice this have deep conviction in these upadeshas; this I pray.

Further, there are many ways of bringing bad conditions to the path in thought and deed. Thus, one should understand them as is taught in the extensive *Seven Points of Mind Training* and so forth. Accordingly, the bodhisattvas practice bringing suffering and destitution to the path.

19

Taking Gain to the Path

Even if I become renowned and everyone pays me respect,
Or should I obtain wealth like that of Vaishravana,
To see the wealth of samsara as having no essence
And not have pride is the practice of a bodhisattva. (19)

If you have amassed an abundance of positive conditions—social status, looks, wealth, youth, and so forth—and are renowned everywhere, many beings may bow down to you with respect. Even if you obtain wealth like Lord Vaishravana[1] or his son, all the wealth of samsara is unstable, like lightning in the sky. It is impermanent, like a drop of dew on a blade of grass. Like a water bubble, it has no essence. Like the skin of a snake, it is an object to be cast away. Regarding it that way, do not have pride or conceit toward whatever wealth and power you may have.

Also, it is said in the sutras:

If one thinks, "I am quite venerable" or "I am the best,"
One will not give rise to bodhichitta.

The *Letter to a Friend* states:

Regard conceit due to class, looks,
Learnedness, youth, and great power to be an enemy.

Should you be well endowed with good qualities such as class, beauty, wealth, power, education, learnedness, and respectability, and, further, should you have great happiness in mind and body, you may, due to arrogance, disregard others and wish to do various non-dharmic deeds. Falling under the power of heedlessness, in this life you will have the various sufferings of getting what you do not want, and in the next life you will take birth as someone of low class or in the lower realms. Such heedlessness is only the cause of the decline of everything in this life and the next. Thus, subdue arrogance and make the aspiration that others have all the conducive worldly and spiritual conditions. In short, acting as the lowest servant to everyone, you should carry everyone on the crown of your head whether they are high or low.

Lord Atisha said:

> Tame and pacify the conceited, arrogant, and prideful mind that denigrates everyone. Give rise to compassion for those who are lower, and abandon disregard and contempt.

Dromtönpa said:

> No matter how many good qualities you may have,
> Lessen your disregard and contempt for others.

Lord Atisha said:

> Do not be disdainful toward those who are not well educated, even down to and including dogs.

Accordingly, the noble ones who came before took a low position. Wearing tattered clothing and so forth, they practiced the dharma. Because of that, they had no pride or conceit.

Chen-ngawa said:

> Son, to the balloon of pride
> The water of good qualities will not stick.

Abandon disregard toward others that comes from the pride of being wealthy, and so forth. It is said that you should believe anything to be beneath you except water.

Patrul Rinpoche said:

Have dislike toward being high and affinity for being low.
With being high comes great pride and jealousy.
With being low, relaxation and virtuous activity grow.
Low positions were the seats of the previous masters.

One should not be conceited about happiness and pleasure and should have
no hope or conceit in relation to high or low positions.
Gyalsepa [Ngulchu Tokmé] said:

> With whatever good qualities of being learned, righteous, and
> good we dharma practitioners may have, we hold ourselves to be
> superior. Due to pride, we have contempt for those who are lower
> than we are, we feel competitive with those who are equal, and
> have jealousy toward those who are higher. All of this misses the
> key point of dharma. Therefore, whomever you spend time with,
> whether they are high, low, or middling, it is said you should
> cherish them, carrying them on the top of your head.

Panchen Chögyen said:

> If we amass wealth and good conditions, through offering generously
> We gather the accumulations. It is easier to be poor than
> Have concern about your wealth going to waste, and the suffering of
>   miserliness.
> A la la! Have equanimity toward wealth and decline.

Accordingly, whether it is gain or loss, happiness or suffering, low or high
rank, whatever should happen to you is suitable. Without having great
pride when things are going well or great loss of heart when things are
not, just train your mind. Moreover, the main point is to understand that
everything—good, bad, happy, sad, wealth, or decline—is like a magical
illusion, a dream. To contemplate this bodhisattva practice is inconceivable!
This is the practice of bringing prosperity to the path.

20

TAKING OBJECTS OF AGGRESSION TO THE PATH

If I do not tame the enemy of my own anger,
I may subdue external enemies, but they will still increase.
Therefore, with the army of loving-kindness and
   compassion,
To tame one's own mind stream is the practice of a
   bodhisattva. (20)

Out of all enemies, the enemy of the intractable mental afflictions—such as aggression in one's mind stream—is extremely difficult to tame. Just as when you put out a fire, smoke will not arise, if you tame the dangerous enemy of the mental afflictions, all outer enemies will naturally become pacified. If you do not tame them, then no matter how many ordinary, outer harmful enemies you tame, they still will proliferate more and more. Since that is so, the great armies of compassion that wish all friends and enemies to be free from suffering, and loving-kindness that wishes them to be happy, will crush the mental afflictions into dust; they have the power to vanquish them into nonexistence.

Also, the *Hundred Verses* states:

Even if you kill all the harm doers that exist,
Enemies will never become exhausted.
If you kill your own anger,
Through that, you will kill all enemies.

Shantideva said:

Unruly beings are [limitless] like the sky:
If you try to eliminate them, you will not succeed.
If you defeat this mind of anger once,
It is like defeating all of them.[1]

Lord Atisha said:

If you tame the inner mind,
Outer enemies cannot harm you.

The strongest army with which to tame this inner enemy is none other than compassion and loving-kindness.

Once, the Three Brothers[2] and a disciple named Khamlungpa went to visit Dromtönpa. Upon arrival, Potowa and the others chatted for a while about how things were. Finally, Dromtönpa asked what Khamlungpa was doing. The others replied that he was sitting inside doing nothing but weeping. Dromtönpa took his hat off, joined his palms together at his heart, and with tears flowing said, "How wondrous he is!" thus praising how the man practiced compassion. "If you could give rise to such uncontrived compassion, you would have the ability to manifestly exchange self for other and to accomplish others' benefit without concern for even your own life."

The genuine dharma, the *Sutra of the Condensed Perfection of Wisdom*, states:

If one engages in many spiritual practices with the desire to attain buddhahood, it will not happen. Practice one, and it will. What is that one? It is great compassion. For those who have great compassion, it is like having all spiritual practices in the palm of their hand.

Yeshe Tsogyal said to Urgyen Rinpoche:

"What is the most wondrous of all dharmas?" she asked. "Bodhichitta is the greatest," he answered. "What is the greatest vehicle of all dharma?" she asked. "Having great compassion is the greatest," he replied.

Accordingly, there are many reasons that show why these two, loving-kindness and compassion, are so important. Previously, in India, even though noble Asanga did the practice of venerable Maitreya, it was due to his compassion that he was finally able to meet Maitreya face to face.[3] There are endless stories like this.

Loving-kindness and compassion are the main practices of the Mahayana path and the root of all dharma. If one has concepts of close and distant and taking others as enemies, the goal [of enlightenment] will not be reached. Therefore, give rise to loving-kindness and compassion that is free from partiality toward all sentient beings in order to pull the poison tree of evil from its root in your mind stream. This is how bodhisattvas bring objects of anger to the path.

21

TAKING OBJECTS OF ATTACHMENT TO THE PATH

The sense pleasures are like salt water:
However much you partake, that much your craving will
increase.
Whatever objects of attachment arise,
To immediately abandon them is the practice of a
bodhisattva. (21)

If you obtain objects of desire—forms, sounds, smells, tastes, and tangible objects that are beautiful, pleasant to hear, fragrant, sweet, soft, and fine, like the sensory enjoyments of the gods—they are like salt water. No matter how much you indulge in them, you will not be satisfied. Suffering and craving will further increase. Attachment to the abundance of samsara is the source of a great many faults in this life and the next. Since that is so, whatever things bring about attachment—wealth and resources in general, or your daily requisites in particular—however pleasing they may be, do not keep them for a long time. In order to hinder your attachment, you should give them up immediately.

The *Udanavarga* says:

Even if money falls like rain,
You will not by satisfied by pleasures.
The learned ones fully understand
The many faults of petty desires.

To get to the very point of it,[1] it is said many times that you should immediately abandon the things you do not wish to give away and whatever you have attachment to.

Also, Lord Atisha said:

Anything you have attachment to you should abandon;
You should remain without attachment.
It is because of attachment that beings cannot achieve happiness,
And so the life force of liberation, too, is cutting attachment.

The teacher of gods and humans[2] said many times, "Immediately abandon attachment. Contentment is supreme among all wealth. It is the noblest wealth. Take this as the essence."

Nagarjuna said:

The teacher of gods and humans said
Among all wealth, contentment is supreme.
Always be satisfied. To the supreme masters,
Not having wealth is the perfect endowment.

In particular, great attachment toward honor, gain, alcohol, spouses and partners, and so forth, will make all forms of awakening, temporary or ultimate, completely unreachable. It goes without saying that for renunciates and mantrikas any type of alcohol is unsuitable. But for laypeople as well, it is unsuitable to drink.

A sutra states:

People who really love to drink alcohol
Are incapable of benefiting themselves or making others happy.
Alcohol makes people ignorant and gives them a bad complexion.
It is just like poison; do not drink it.

And:

Drinking alcohol made from grain, which makes one euphoric
and makes one heedless, is included within the thirty-five faults
of heedlessness.

Then:

> You should know that is how it is.

There are a great number of faults that are mentioned up to that point.
The *Application of Mindfulness Sutra* states:

> People who depend on alcohol
> Are the axe of all dharma.

And:

> When one drinks delicious alcohol
> [The negative qualities] ripen intensely.

The Vinaya says:

> If one drinks alcohol, one is born in the Hell of Weeping,
> And the one who serves such alcohol will be born close by.

The *Sutra of Revealing of What Is Virtuous and Unvirtuous* states:

> Drunkards and drinkers of alcohol in this life will be born in the
> hell where one drinks hot molten copper.

Statements like these are innumerable.
    As such sayings are said in the context of the sutras and the *pratimoksha*,[3]
you may wonder if they are appropriate in the context of the Mantrayana:[4]
The *Tantra of Purifying the Lower Realms* states:

> Do not drink alcohol.
> Also do not eat meat, and so forth.

The *Vajra Pinnacle* states:

> The root of all destruction is
> Alcohol; abandon it completely.

This is said many times.

If you wonder whether or not it is suitable to have meat and alcohol in the context of feast ceremonies[5] of the highest yoga tantra, the *Kalachakra Tantra* says:

It is for the purpose of offering homage to vajra speech, but for practitioners of mantra, intoxicants are not to be drunk.

One may say, "Well, one should properly obtain the samaya substances in accord [with the instructions]; not adhering to this would be a contradiction." To reply to that statement, the main samaya substances are the five meats and the five *amritas*.[6] If someone does not have the capability to partake of horse meat, human meat, feces, urine, or anything with a rotten odor, then they just give alcohol the name "amrita." Their three gates remain ordinary; they cannot control their thoughts; they engage in the five poisons and keep the conduct of dogs and swine. Moreover, those with such arrogant false perception about the samaya substances and amrita only have the cause of despair.

Dromtönpa said:

For mantrikas, regarding alcohol as important is not a samaya.

As to so-called amrita, since it vanquishes the five poisons, the afflictive emotions, it is called a [powerful] demon. It is the elixir of the expansion of great bliss, primordial wisdom. You should understand this. Those who came before—the great beings who went beyond to the stage of accomplishment— when they partook of alcohol, they did it at appropriate times. They were not obscured by ordinary thoughts; whatever appeared to them arose as the deity. Because they gained mastery in the two truths, they were able to attract others who had confidence in the view. They were able to transform water into alcohol and poison into medicine. If one tried to imitate them, it would be like a fox trying to imitate a lion. When one has craving for alcohol and then partakes of it, the power of any good qualities of hearing and meditating that one may have are veiled like the darkness of a deep crevice. Ultimately it cannot go beyond being anything but the cause of the lower realms.

Jetsun Milarepa said:

Alcohol is the substance of the craving of sense pleasures.
If you drink it, you will cut the life vein of liberation.

Urgyen Rinpoche said:

One aspect of the cause of the suffering of the three realms of samsara is alcohol. Should you encounter it, do not drink it. Abandon it. When you give rise to the six expressive energies of primordial wisdom, alcohol clouds them over with the sleep of ignorance. When you are guarding the vows that you have taken, alcohol makes you careless. When the wisdom being[7] becomes clear, alcohol makes the five poisons burn like fire.

Many statements such as this have been made.

Since the Buddha, the teacher, prophesied that alcohol would be the destroyer of his teaching, we all should be heedful. Since the root of all inducers of flaws and afflictions arises from this, you should not have great craving for alcohol and should abandon it.

Similarly, since the consumption of meat also hinders all of the higher and lower vehicles, the sutras state:

For the sake of profit, sentient beings are killed.
For the sake of meat, money is paid.
Both of these entail negative karma.
They are the main accumulation for those in the Wailing Hell.

And:

Also, one of the twenty-five hardships mentioned in the Kalachakra empowerments is not to eat meat that was killed or to drink alcohol.

Such things are said many times.

In particular, in the tradition of the great vehicle of bodhisattvas, one should be a refuge and protect all the limitless sentient beings. Heartlessly killing sentient beings who have negative karma—the objects of protection—and, having promised to protect them, heedlessly eating them is a fault of completely lacking scrutiny. These days, not only do people not give up meat, they don't even say the *dharani* mantra[8] of the buddhas and bodhisattvas [before they eat it]. Not having the mindfulness to bless the food is extremely improper. Not only that, there is no way the victorious ones will be pleased by offerings of meat and blood that arrogantly assume virtue and the benefit of others.

Shantideva said:

> Just as someone completely immersed in fire
> Is unmoved by any object of pleasure,
> Likewise, if we harm sentient beings,
> There is no way to please the great compassionate ones.[9]

Likewise, you should abandon spouses and partners as well. The sutras say:

> In the three-thousand-fold universe
> There is no enemy like one's spouse.
> There is no prison like samsara.
> There is no prison guard like your relatives.

The Great One from Uddiyana said:

> Due to their dark intentions, romantic partners are called "dark."
> Because they are removed from society, they are called "removed."
> They are called "devoid" since they are without virtuous mind.

Vairochana said:

> The deeds of romantic partners are poison;
> Sentient beings who ingest it will surely die.
> They are the agents of the anguish of evil spirits.
> Whoever relates with them will experience measureless suffering.

As for attachment and desire toward romantic partners, if you do not get away from this single foundation of all suffering and samsara, it will be the source of much deceit and cunning. It is the main thing to be abandoned, as it is cited in the scriptures many times, as in stories such as those of Angulimala who killed 999 men[10] and of Vairochana who was exiled.[11] "With one hundred tugs upward, it won't come up, but with a single dip, down it goes."[12] As this saying illustrates, lamas, *khenpos*, *acharyas*, dharma friends, parents, and so on who teach about virtue and nonvirtue, what to adopt and abandon, and about the present and subsequent lifetimes, no matter how much they explain faults and good qualities, people do not listen to them. But when a single person seen as attractive merely shows a smile, what use is there talking about what will happen in the next life, when in this life, some are like dogs that follow around humans, not remembering even to appear to have some sense of decency. Beings [easily] become completely separated from the path of liberation and omniscience. That is the cause of going to the lower realms, just like a stone being thrown into a great ocean. You should completely abandon such conduct.

If that is so, then are meat, alcohol, and partners to be abandoned even in the context of the secret Mantrayana? When the time is not appropriate for them, you should completely abandon them.

A *Great Perfection Tantra* says:

This conduct is connected with a particular time.

This is illustrated in the story of a past Indian siddha named Nagpopa, who was a master in the practice of Chakrasamvara. However, because of his untimely fault, he encountered obstacles.[13]

Not only that, the elder Bödung said:

If one bestows a true empowerment[14] to a student who is not ready, the student will die from bleeding and vomiting. [The one who bestows the empowerment] also will die, and so forth. If, for someone who has realization, the five poisons increase greatly and it makes them become careless and wild, what need is there to say anything about someone like us? Likewise, a crow will die if it thinks it can compete with a peacock and eat poison the way a peacock does.[15] Having once obtained this human birth, you should make it meaningful and not fall under the sway of confusion.

Dakpo Rinpoche[16] said:

First, the bringer of negativity is various types of meat.
Second, the intoxicator is golden beer.
Third, the deceiver is acquaintance with other partners.
These three are the deadly poisons of dharma.
The practitioner of the stainless dharma abandons these three.

Drupwang Kalden Gyamtso said:

Due to craving for delicious food,
Attachment to soft clothing,
And desire for beautiful bodies,
You will forget the way of the profound dharma.

Accordingly, all the qualities of attachment, desire, and craving are like drinking salt water; one is never satisfied. Partaking of such poison is a definite cause of unhappiness. To immediately abandon it is the bodhisattva practice of bringing objects of pleasure and craving to the path.

22

MEDITATIVE EQUIPOISE FREE FROM
CLINGING TO ELABORATIONS

Whatever appears is one's own mind.
Mind is primordially free from extremes of elaboration.
Knowing this is so, to not mentally engage
The signs of perceiver and perceived is the practice of a
    bodhisattva. (22)

Whatever appears—outer and inner phenomena, the world and its
contents—all of it is merely imputed by one's own mind. Since it is not established from its own side, it is empty. The nature of this mind that imputes is
primordially free from all extremes of elaboration such as existence, nonexistence, eternalism, and nihilism. In that way, the abiding nature of all phenomena, which are subsumed in subject and object, is ultimately suchness.
Understanding this, to not apprehend any characteristics or elaborations
that cling to thinking, "Outer objects and the inner perceiving mind truly
exist" is the meditation of emptiness, free of elaboration, the equipoise that
is like space.

Also, the *Prajnaparamita* states:

Knowing that all phenomena are of the nature of emptiness, with no
    arising,
Is the conduct of the supreme prajnaparamita.

All appearances, apart from being phenomena produced by one's mind, are
not established as something else; not even a mere atom exists. For example,

no matter what may appear in your dream at night, when you wake up there is nothing that exists apart from mind's confusion.

The siddha Lingchenrepa said:

> Mind itself, which is without base or root,
> Is like the experience of last night's dream.
> Do you understand that this is the master
> Pointing out that appearances are mind?

The *Lamp for the Path of Awakening* states:

> Phenomena are the confusion of mind.
> There are no phenomena that do not arise from mind.

Accordingly, the mind does not exist as being identifiable as "this." It does not go beyond the nature of emptiness.

It is also said:

> When one looks inwardly at one's own mind,
> Mind is not seen as "this."
> This "not seeing" is seeing the dharma.
> This is the ground of all the buddhas.

Accordingly, the empty essence of mind is not established anywhere. For example, like the center of unobstructed space, it is free from arising, abiding, and ceasing. All phenomena are established in themselves vividly and distinctly as the nature of the unceasing energetic display. Outer apprehended objects are not established as being any essence at all.[1] With respect to the inner apprehending mind, do not grasp onto anything whatsoever such as it being a thing or a non-thing.

The Fifth Dalai Lama said:

> All phenomena, being alpha-pure, cannot be found; they are empty.
> Although they are empty, they clearly appear, like illusions.
> When one sees the essence of appearances, nothing can be identified.
> Although they don't exist, all happiness and suffering can be
>   experienced.

Thus, do not conceptually examine reality. Do not analyze it. Without fixating on anything, free of elaborations, you should rest directly, naturally settled.

Lord Atisha said:

> Within the *dharmata* that is free from elaborations,
> Let cognition also rest, free from elaborations.

The Great One from Uddiyana said to the Self-Arising Queen:[2]

> When you meditate, there is nothing whatsoever. It is empty.
> If, distracted, you follow after and cling to outer appearances, you are deluded.
> Having analyzed and examined, sustain it without adopting or rejecting.
> There is nothing to meditate on, but there is training to be stabilized.

Accordingly, without meditating and without being distracted, to rest free from mental elaborations is the bodhisattva practice of equipoise that meditates on emptiness like space.

23

ABANDONING TAKING OBJECTS OF
ATTACHMENT AS TRULY EXISTENT

Encountering pleasurable objects
Is like seeing a rainbow in the summertime.
Although they appear beautiful and real, to see them as not
    being real
And relinquish attachment is the practice of a bodhisattva. (23)

Pleasurable objects that you encounter, such as your friends and relatives, beautiful forms and sounds, happiness, and those things that bring happiness, apart from merely appearing do not exist. They are just like a beautiful, vividly appearing rainbow in the summertime. Whatever beautiful or pleasant self-appearances you have, do not cling to them as being truly existent. See them as not being truly real. Thinking, "This is beautiful and this is ugly; this is someone close to me; this is a friend," abandon attachment that fixates on taking things as real from their own side. This is the bodhisattva practice of ceasing clinging to the true existence of desirable objects.

24

ABANDONING TAKING OBJECTS OF
AVERSION AS TRULY EXISTENT

The different kinds of suffering are like your child dying in a
dream.
Taking confused appearances as real, how tiring!
Therefore, when meeting with adverse conditions,
To see them as confusion is the practice of a bodhisattva.
(24)

Unpleasant objects that may come to you—such as ghosts, ugly forms, unpleasant sounds, suffering, that which brings suffering, and the various types of undesirable objects—are just like the analogy of the death of your cherished child in a dream: although there is the appearance of the experience of suffering, in fact it is not existent. Taking suffering and confused appearances to be real in this way is so tiring! It brings the suffering of being weary and disheartened. Therefore, when you meet with adverse and difficult situations, you should look upon them and think, "Apart from these being merely confused appearances, not even a fraction of them exists as real on its own."

Also, the *King of Samadhi Sutra* states:

The illusory forms conjured by magicians—
Horses, elephants, and chariots—
Appearances are like that; none of them exist.
Understand all phenomena to be like that.

And:

> Just as a young lady who, in her dreams,
> Sees a son born and then die
> Is happy at his birth and unhappy with his death,
> Understand all phenomena to be like that.

Lord Atisha said:

> When attachment or anger toward something arises,
> Regard that thing as the conjuring of a magician.

Kharakpa said:

> All phenomena are like a dream or an illusion.
> There is not even a single thing that is real.
> Things appear while not existing,
> So do not become attached to things!

In that way, if you do intense meditation on emptiness while in meditative equipoise, during postmeditation all appearances will naturally arise as dreams and illusions. If your realization in meditative equipoise is slight, during postmeditation you should rely on strong mindfulness to foster the view of seeing things as illusory. Not only that, through meditation on emptiness in meditative equipoise, during postmeditation, if you have compassion for sentient beings and develop confidence in actions and their results, you will implicitly engage in the accumulations of wisdom and merit.

Rinchen Gangpapa said:

> Those who are bound by clinging to things as real
> Will not gain the two accumulations of the levels.[1]
> Thus, the dharma of having no attachment to appearances,
> [Seeing things] as an illusion, is very important.

The lord guru also said:

> The space-like emptiness of meditative equipoise
> And the illusion-like emptiness of postmeditation:

Meditating on them, the bodhisattvas are praiseworthy,
For their transcendent conduct embodies the union of means and
wisdom.

Thus, however you conduct yourself in postmeditation, it is said you should
know that phenomena are not real; [be] like a child of illusion, without
being separated from the experience of meditative equipoise. Accordingly,
meditating upon everything as illusory without taking the object of attachment or anger to be real in postmeditation is the practice of a bodhisattva.

25

THE MEANS OF GENEROSITY

Since, if you wish for enlightenment, you must give even
   your body away,
What is there to be said about giving material objects to
   others?
Therefore, to have generosity without hope of
Being paid in return is the practice of a bodhisattva. (25)

In order to attain perfect buddhahood, great enlightenment, as it said in
the *Jataka Tales*:

> If the head or limbs or even the whole body must be given count-
> less times for the benefit of others, what need is there to say any-
> thing about having to give objects of material wealth, spouses,
> children, and so forth, to others. Therefore, train in the practice
> of generosity, unadulterated by self-interest—the hope that mate-
> rial wealth will be returned to you in this life, and the striving
> for the ripening of great wealth in the next life. One should give
> in this way, taking hold of the special generous attitude that has
> the results of the roots of virtue of the three types of generosity.

Further, the *Entrance* states:[1]

> To give is the paramita of generosity.

Jamgön Lama said:

The wish-fulfilling jewel, generosity, the fulfiller of the hopes of
  beings,
Is the supreme weapon that cuts through the knot of miserliness.
Giving rise to courage without losing heart is the conduct of
  bodhisattvas.
It is the basis of renown in the ten directions.
Understanding this, the wise rely on the excellent path
Of giving away their body, possessions, and virtue.

The subcategories of generosity are (1) the generosity of material goods; (2) the generosity of dharma; and (3) the generosity of protection from fear.

For the first, the generosity of material goods, there is giving, great giving, and extraordinary giving.

THE GENEROSITY OF MATERIAL GOODS

Giving

Here the practice is to give one's possessions to others, even as little as a tiny package of tea or a cupful of grain. If your intention in doing that is completely pure, then the size of the object is not important.

The *Sutra of the Three Parts*[2] says that even giving just a morsel of food to one born as an animal is virtuous.

If you hold on to your possessions until you die, you are not able to use them for the sake of this life or the next. Thinking you have nothing, no matter how much you have, and ranting about that is a concordant cause for rebirth as a hungry ghost. Rather than doing that, you should strive to be generous and make offerings.

The Vinaya states:

If you do not practice generosity, then you will not have wealth.
You will be completely powerless to magnetize sentient beings.
What is there to say about attaining enlightenment?

Practicing dharma by giving possessions and objects, it is said, was mainly taught to lay bodhisattvas. Monastics train only in having few desires and cultivating contentment. For such monastic practitioners to put into practice the three trainings of the superior path by keeping to mountain retreats and monasteries with determination is very important. Regarding monastics who break their virtuous conduct and have the conceit of offering others material possessions acquired through negativity and cunning, such as business or farming, it is said:

> If you do not practice dharma that is in accord with dharma,
> then dharma will become the cause of the lower realms.

Great Giving

Great giving is giving to others things that you consider highly valuable, such as horses, oxen, jewels, and various types of rare things.

Extraordinary Giving

Extraordinary giving means giving one's life and body, such as when Prince Mahasattva[3] gave his body to the tigress and when Nagarjuna gave his own head to the prosperous prince.[4] Such actions are the conduct of beings who have attained the levels and not for us ordinary beings to practice. Now, without attachment, dedicate your life and body for the sake of sentient beings and make the aspiration that in the next life you will actually be able to give up your life for other beings.

THE GENEROSITY OF DHARMA

The generosity of dharma refers to bestowing empowerments and giving dharma discourses and reading transmissions for the sake of others as a method for joining their mind streams with virtue. However, until we extinguish our own self-interest, our intention to accomplish benefit for the sake of others will merely be an imitation. The virtuous teachers of the past, the Three Brothers,[5] asked, "Of the two, meditating in isolated places and teaching the dharma that benefits sentient beings, which is more profitable?"

The teacher[6] said: A beginner who has not a single bit of experience or realization cannot benefit others through dharma. It is like trying to pour blessings from an empty container; the blessings will not come. Their oral instructions will be like beer without any yeast added. It will be flavorless. A person who is on the path of accumulation and does not have stability in having obtained "heat"[7] cannot benefit sentient beings. It is like pouring from a blessing vase that is full; if you simply fill someone else's, your own becomes empty. The oral instructions are like holding a butter lamp; if you merely provide illumination for another, then you yourself are left in darkness. If you obtain the levels, then you will accomplish whatever you set out to accomplish for those beings that are lower than you in terms of spiritual practice. Such persons are like a blessing vase of excellent siddhi: even if due to that [teaching] others become ripened, you yourself will remain full. The oral instructions are like the main butter lamp:[8] even though one brings illumination to others, one is not kept in darkness oneself. Therefore, in this polluted age, ordinary beings should, in solitary places, train in loving-kindness, compassion, and bodhichitta.

The Indian Padampa Sangye said:

> Since it is said, "The source of wealth is the dharma," until your own desires are exhausted,[9] do not hurry to benefit others. When you say prayers, do recitations, read the scriptures of the Victorious One, and so forth, the pure ones will listen and in turn will make aspirations for liberation; this is said to be satisfactory.[10]

THE GENEROSITY OF PROTECTION FROM FEAR

The generosity of protection from fear means giving courage, refuge, and protection, without bias, to those sentient beings without refuge or protector and to those without courage or friends. In particular, protecting the lives of others is of great benefit.

The Teacher said:

> Of all composite virtues,[11] protecting the life of a single being is the greatest.

Accordingly, if one summarizes all the good qualities of the three types of generosity into a single key point, Yeshe Tsogyal said to Padmasambhava:

> "Why should one practice the paramita of generosity?" [Padmasambhava answered:] "Because it makes one free from avarice."

As to the faults of grasping and the benefits of giving, the *Condensed Paramita Sutra* states:

> By being generous, one will not be clutched by the mental afflictions.
> By grasping, one will develop them; it is not the path of the noble ones.

The Fifth Dalai Lama said:

> With a generous mind, give your body and wealth
> To beings whose kindness cannot be repaid.
> Through generosity of countless aeons, you will accomplish here and now
> The inexhaustible treasury of the wealth of lasting happiness.

This is taught to be the bodhisattva training of the paramita of generosity.

26

THE MEANS OF DISCIPLINE

If, lacking discipline, you do not accomplish your own
benefit,
Wishing to accomplish others' benefit is laughable!
Therefore, to engage in discipline
Without samsaric craving is the practice of a bodhisattva. (26)

If you do not accomplish even the higher realms for yourself and go to the
lower realms without keeping the pure discipline that you committed to,
your wishing to help others to attain perfect enlightenment is laughable.
Therefore, without samsaric attachment or craving, be free of the corrupted
intention of striving for a body in the higher realms of humans, gods, and so
forth. In order to accomplish perfect enlightenment for the sake of others,
you should maintain focus and excellently keep the three types of discipline.

Also, the *Entrance to the Middle Way* says:

If someone breaks the foot of discipline,
Even if they have the wealth of generosity, they will plunge into the
lower realms.

Even though someone has generosity, if they do not have discipline, they will
not obtain the riches of the pure bodies of gods and humans. Moreover, if
they do not have discipline, they will not be liberated from samsara:
The sutras say:

How can someone with no feet go on the path?
Just so, if you do not have discipline, you will not be liberated.

Lord Atisha said:

The beauty of this life and the happiness of the next life come from always having perfect discipline.

There are three subcategories of discipline: (1) the discipline of the vows to refrain from harm; (2) the discipline of gathering virtue; (3) and the discipline of acting for the benefit of beings.

THE DISCIPLINE OF THE VOWS OF REFRAINING FROM HARM

For the first type, there are the general vows and particular vows. The general vows consist of discipline in relation to others, such as the seven types of pratimoksha vows[1]—taking ordination and so forth—whereby one abandons all nonvirtue of the three gates, the basis of harm; [here, the main emphasis is] turning away from harming others for one's own benefit. Specifically, these vows consist mainly of abandoning the seven nonvirtues of body and speech.

The particular vows kept by bodhisattvas are mainly the vows of body, speech, and mind and are encompassed in all of the ten unvirtuous actions. Bodhisattvas turn away from doing harm for the sake of others. In that way, in the context of the bodhisattva vows, if one is not free from attachment to any external or internal desires, all of the vows will implicitly become corrupted. What could be said of performing the benefit of others in any respect, directly or indirectly? One would be unable to benefit even oneself.

The *Prajnaparamita Sutras*[2] state:

If, due to desire, one is cut off from being born in the Abode of Brahma,[3] what is there to say about unsurpassable, perfect complete enlightenment?

Potowa said:

To give an analogy for the discipline of keeping vows: a pestle will churn as much as will be done by the hand of the person holding it. If they cast it away, it will go where it is thrown. If they put it down, it will stay where it is placed. The nonvirtue of our body and speech is like the pestle; body and speech do not have power

over where the mind steers them. Since mind is the doer of everything, emphasize developing control over the mind.[4]

It is said:

> If you wish to protect your training,
> With utter concentration, guard your mind.
> If you do not guard your mind,
> You cannot guard your training.

In all activities, it is through mindfulness and heedfulness that the vows
are kept.

THE DISCIPLINE OF GATHERING VIRTUE

Once you have taken on the discipline of the bodhisattva vows for the sake
of enlightenment, whatever virtue of body and speech you accumulate is, in
brief, the discipline of gathering virtue. Why is that?
The *Bodhisattvabhumi* states:

> Depend upon and abide within the discipline of a bodhisattva.
> Strive joyfully only in listening, contemplating, and meditating.
> Attend and honor gurus. Attend the sick and nurse them. Pro-
> claim others' excellent generosity and qualities. Delight in the
> merit of others and have patience with their contempt. Dedi-
> cate virtue toward enlightenment and make aspirations. Make
> offerings to the three jewels and engage in diligence. Maintain
> heedfulness. Remember the trainings. With attentiveness, guard
> your mind. Guard the gates of the sense faculties and take food
> in moderation. In the first and the last parts of the night, do not
> sleep but diligently engage in yogic practice. Rely on holy beings
> and spiritual friends. Having examined your own confusion,
> confess and relinquish it. Accomplishing such dharma activities,
> guard them and make them increase extensively. Understand
> this to be the discipline of gathering virtue.

Accordingly, if virtuous dharma, such as the six paramitas, has not arisen
in your mind stream, give rise to it. Once it has been embraced, do not let it
diminish, but strive to make it increase.

Potowa said:

> For example, just as all objects arise and are held together due
> to moisture, it is said that the six paramitas give rise to and hold
> together all phenomena that are the cause for buddhahood. All
> virtues are accomplished through the six paramitas.

THE DISCIPLINE OF BENEFITING SENTIENT BEINGS

You should behave only in ways that either directly or indirectly benefit
beings. In order for your virtue not to decline and for others to have faith
in you, you should abandon impure actions of the three gates and keep to
pure actions of the three gates. Abandon unruly conduct of the body such
as jumping and running. Have a tamed demeanor in all daily activities such
as walking, sitting, eating, and sleeping, and avoid sharp speech or speaking
too much. In a state of ease and loving-kindness, smile. Do not become
engrossed in personal honor and gain or in drowsiness, and so forth. If you
remember faith and compassion and so on, you will abide with wisdom.

Further, the *Bodhisattvabhumi* states:

> Through meaningful deeds such as making friends; showing the
> way to those who do not know the method; returning benefit to
> others with a sense of gratitude; protecting from fears; dispelling
> suffering and anguish; obtaining daily necessities for those who
> do not have them; excellently gathering dharma disciples; help-
> ing those who are ready to enter the dharma; taking pleasure
> in the qualities that are perfectly pure; perfectly subjugating
> wrong views; through magic, instilling fear in [those who must
> be tamed]; and inspiring others. . . .

The twelve points[5] above have been set out as a summary [for how to engage
in the discipline of benefiting others]. In this way, whatever is suitable for
benefiting sentient beings, you should accomplish it.

Potowa said:

> All the parents there are in the world, without caring for their
> own body or even their own life, help their child as much as they

can and never tire of bringing them benefit. Like that, directly or indirectly, you should also benefit sentient beings.

Similarly, through training in abandoning negative deeds and practicing virtue, and also through adopting the three excellences,[6] dedicate that for the benefit of sentient beings. Either directly or indirectly, accomplish only benefit for others in many ways. Thus, the three types of discipline are the basis of all qualities.

Lord Atisha said:

Engage in the discipline that strives in what to adopt and reject.
It is the basis of the source of all qualities without exception.

Yeshe Tsogyal said to Guru Rinpoche:

"What is the paramita of discipline?" He answered, "It is the mind being free from stains."

Kharakpa said:

The cause for obtaining the human birth with the freedoms and resources
Is the precious training of discipline.
You must guard whatever stainless qualities
Have been obtained in your mind stream!

THE FAULTS OF WANING DISCIPLINE

The *Prajnaparamita Sutras* states:

If, because of having poor discipline, one does not have the ability to benefit oneself, then what is there to say about helping someone else? The ripening of poor discipline is being reborn as a hell being, in the animal realm, or in Yama's[7] domain.

THE BENEFICIAL QUALITIES OF KEEPING DISCIPLINE

The *Letter to a Friend* says:

> Just like the earth is the basis of all that moves and is unmoving,
> Discipline is taught to be the basis of all good qualities.

There are many [teachings], such as the way of practicing, on the special discipline that serves as the cause for liberation and omniscience.

Accordingly, since the three kinds of discipline accomplish perfect enlightenment for the benefit of others, one should keep them perfectly. This is the bodhisattvas' practice of training in the paramita of discipline.

27

THE MEANS OF PATIENCE

For bodhisattvas who desire a wealth of virtue,
All harmful actions done to them are like a precious treasure.
Therefore, to practice patience that is
Without any malice toward anyone is the practice of a
    bodhisattva. (27)

The supreme of all hardships is practicing patience. Thus, for bodhisattvas who desire to engage in a vast wealth of virtue, whatever brings harm, such as enemies or suffering, is like the bursting-forth of an inexhaustible treasure in your own home, a great field of rare precious jewels, difficult to find, that you did not know about. Therefore, without even the slightest thought of anger or ill will toward anyone who inflicts harm, you should practice the three types of patience.

Further, the *Bodhisattvapitaka Sutra* states:

Anger vanquishes the root of virtue that has been accumulated
for a hundred thousand aeons.

Even if someone has both generosity and discipline, if they do not have patience, anger will arise. If you become angry, all the virtues that were previously accumulated—generosity, discipline, and so on—will be destroyed in a single instant.

The *Entrance to the Way of a Bodhisattva* states:

All of these excellent practices,
Such as generosity and offerings to the buddhas

That are accumulated over a thousand aeons,
Will be vanquished by even a single moment of anger.[1]

Accordingly, there are three types of patience: (1) patience toward others' ingratitude; (2) the patience of enduring hardships for the sake of the dharma; and (3) the patience of not fearing profound reality.

Patience toward Others' Ingratitude

Whatever the source of anger may be, whether others directly beat and rob you, make various insults, or secretly say unkind things about you, you should develop patience and tolerance. Should you allow your anger to be unleashed, it is said that through a single moment of anger, the accumulation of merit of one thousand aeons will be vanquished. It is a great negativity.
   As it is said:

There is no negativity like anger.
There is no fortitude like patience.
Since that is so, in various ways,
Persistently practice patience.[2]

Accordingly, remembering the faults of anger, you should strive to practice patience at all times and in all situations.
   The Indian sage Padampa Sangye said:

Enemies are the confused appearances of karma.
People of Dingri, transform your poisonous mind of anger toward them.

Right now, if you have patience and do not hold on to resentment or become angry over unkind words or abuse, you will also perfect an immense accumulation of merit. Without objects that trigger your anger, I ask, how can you practice patience? For us who presume to be dharma practitioners, the sign that the dharma has arisen in our mind stream is that our body, speech, and mind become soft and quieted, just like cotton cloth gets matted down from being stepped on.
   Otherwise, with one's mind stream distracted due to having arrogance and pride over having engaged in only a little bit of hearing, meditating,

and keeping the various vows, one's mind stream and dharma become separate, and one reels with anger merely at another's insults. This is a sign that dharma has not been of the slightest benefit to one's mind.

Chen-ngawa said:

> If we who have engaged in hearing, contemplating, and meditating develop our ego further, our fortitude in patience will lessen and become softened like the new skin of a wound that is healing. Being tightly fixated on irritations[3] is the sign of having turned away from hearing, contemplating, and meditating.

Compared to even a thousand profound meditations and high views that do not benefit the mind, the single practice of patience—not getting angry—is extremely profound.

THE PATIENCE OF ENDURING HARDSHIP FOR THE SAKE OF THE DHARMA

In order to practice the genuine dharma, you must practice disregarding all the hardships of heat and cold.

The tantras say:

> [Even if you have to] cross an ocean of blazing-hot razors,
> Until you reach the next life, seek out the genuine dharma.

Of all the great beings who came before, in the writings of the Kadampas, Kagyus, and so forth, as well as in their life stories, there was no one who accomplished the dharma through happiness, well-being, and renown. Accordingly, if we hope to accomplish dharma while in a state of happiness, well-being, and renown, without the need for even the slightest bit of tenacity or hardship in pursuing it, then before we even start practicing dharma, we invite the maras.[4]

Rigpe Wangchuk said:

> Without even engaging in a single dharma practice,
> You arrogantly see yourself as a dharma practitioner. Oh, how foolish!
> The first step of dharma practice is to relinquish this life.
> Look to see whether that is in your mind stream or not.

146 — THE EXCELLENT VASE OF NECTAR

Lord Atisha said:

"The Four Aims of the Kadampas" are:
Aim your mind toward the dharma. Aim your dharma practice at simple living.[5] Aim at simple living until death. Aim to die
in solitude.[6] Make only engaging in these hardships your main
practice. Even if there were an individual superior to our teacher
[the Buddha], still, there would be no way to take up dharma
and worldly activity together. Even though the Buddha was a
chakravartin king,[7] he abandoned worldly activity like spit from
the mouth. Because of his dedication and undergoing hardships
for six years on the banks of the river Nairanjana, he found the
way to realize his intention. If we ordinary people who follow
him do not engage in the dharma with dedication and hardship,
how could there be any way to attain enlightenment?

Potawa said:

If fishermen, outcastes, and farmers
Endure sufferings such as heat and cold
While thinking merely of their livelihood,
What is there to say about undergoing hardship for the dharma?

Accordingly, for the sake of ultimate enlightenment, you should continuously develop great confidence from the depths of your heart with respect to
tenacity and enduring hardship for the sake of the genuine dharma.

THE PATIENCE OF NOT FEARING PROFOUND REALITY

If one does not have faith in the nature of emptiness of the two selves, the
reality of suchness, and in particular, if one hears such teachings as the
Eight Great Words of Wonder or the *Twelve Vajra Laughs*[8] that [teach] the
Great Perfection—the natural state that is free of effort and activity and is
beyond virtue, nonvirtue, karma, cause, and effect—and then, regarding
them erroneously, slanders them, accumulating intensely negative karma,
such a person will stay in the vajra hell for countless aeons.
As it is said:

One with the severe negative karma of the five inexpiable misdeeds
Should confess that accumulated negative karma of abandoning
dharma.

Before, during the time of the Buddha, upon hearing the teaching on the
meaning of profound emptiness, many prideful monks vomited blood, died,
and were reborn in a hell realm. There are a number of such stories.
Lord Atisha also said:

Having trained the mind through loving-kindness, compassion,
and bodhichitta, if one doesn't have any confidence in the profound dharma [of emptiness] and only keeps the vows purely, one
cannot go anywhere, it is said.

Accordingly, one should have earnest devotion toward the profound
dharma and the people who teach it. Even if, under the sway of one's own
small-mindedness, one does not take that on, it is important at least to give
up deprecating [the dharma and those who teach it]. On top of practicing
the three types of patience, to summarize and combine them into a single
point along with the ways of bringing adverse conditions to the path as
explained above, as Lord Atisha said:

The supreme patience is holding oneself in a low position.

The Fifth Dalai Lama said:

In preparation for battle with the army of afflictions,
When one dons the fierce, excellent armor of patience,
One escapes to the place beyond torment, unpierced
By weapons, harsh words, and beatings. How wonderful!

THE FAULTS OF ANGER

It is said:

The result of the accumulations of merit of a thousand aeons
Is vanquished by a single moment of anger.

In particular, in all your births your complexion will be bad, and you will have an ugly, unpleasant form, such as having horns. You will be born only with a body that has an unpleasant odor. Thus, it is important to be very careful not to have the great negativity of anger and aggression.

THE BENEFITS OF PATIENCE

The *Entrance to the Way of a Bodhisattva* states:

> Whoever assiduously subdues their anger
> Will have joy in this and other lives.[9]

Patience is the single root of all happiness in this and subsequent lives, and of temporary and ultimate benefit and happiness. In particular, [if you have patience,] in all your births you will be beautiful and pleasing. The Buddha also said that being ornamented with the [thirty-two] auspicious marks is the benefit of having patience. Since there is nothing of greater benefit than the patience of enduring hardship, to persevere in having patience is very important. This is the bodhisattvas' practice of training in the paramita of patience.

28

THE MEANS OF DILIGENCE

Though the hearers and solitary realizers practice only for
their own benefit,
They exert themselves like their hair is on fire.
Seeing this, to practice diligence, the source of qualities,
For the sake of all beings is the practice of a bodhisattva. (28)

The hearers and solitary realizers wish to accomplish mere peace solely for
their own benefit. They practice on the path the way someone whose hair and
clothes have caught fire strives to quickly put it out. Seeing such diligence, what
need is there to say that one [on the bodhisattva path] should engage in vast
diligence toward the source of all qualities, the immense conduct of bodhisattvas that gives rise to supreme enlightenment for the sake of all beings? To
do that, train in the three kinds of diligence in order to accomplish perfect
enlightenment. Furthermore, someone who has generosity and so forth but
does not have diligence is lazy. If you have laziness, you will not accomplish
virtue, will not be able to benefit others, and will not attain enlightenment.
The *Request of Sagaramati Sutra* states:

Lazy ones are devoid of [the six paramitas] from generosity to
wisdom. Lazy ones will not benefit others. For lazy ones, enlightenment is extremely far away.

Sakya Pandita said:

For a lazy person, even drinking water is too much work.

If he said this, what is there to say about practicing dharma?

Laziness [can be divided into three types]: the laziness of sloth, the laziness of discouragement, and the laziness of useless deeds. The laziness of sloth is attachment to the comfort of a languorous mind, such as sleeping, lying down, and torpor. The laziness of discouragement is when someone without impaired faculties becomes disheartened, thinking, "How could a person like me attain enlightenment even through effort?" The laziness of useless deeds is having attachment to nonvirtue such as accumulating wealth, protecting close ones, and conquering enemies for the sake of this life. Since these are the direct cause of suffering, they should be avoided. You should rely on the antidote to laziness, which is diligence.

Shantideva said:

Diligence is delight in virtue.[1]

Accordingly, diligence can be divided into three: (1) armor-like diligence; (2) applied diligence; and (3) insatiable diligence.

Armor-Like Diligence

Armor-like diligence means that from this time forth until placing all sentient beings in unsurpassable enlightenment, one thinks, "I will not give up diligence in practicing virtue!" thus wearing it like armor.

The *Bodhisattvapitaka Sutra* states:

Shariputra, don the inconceivable armor. Until the very end of samsara, for the sake of enlightenment, do not slacken your diligence.

Thus, without considering their own bodies and lives, the bodhisattvas who came before adopted the conduct of not thinking anything of hardship in making efforts for the sake of each individual sentient being. If we analyze this: at this time, each of us has been weighed down by the burden of our negative karma; why would someone who has, since beginningless time, developed no positive habits from former training not need determination and endurance in hardship? Now you have attained a human birth that has the freedoms and resources in order to benefit others with the excellent intention that does not consider oneself. At this time when you have encountered a qualified guru, make a heartfelt commitment, thinking, "Why should I not practice the genuine dharma?"

Potowa said:

> The diligence of the bodhisattvas does not refer to the ordinary actions of body and speech. It is delighting in benefiting others and is called "armor" and "great fortitude."

APPLIED DILIGENCE

Applied diligence is persevering in abandoning all nonvirtue that is motivated by the afflictions—attachment and so forth—and striving in virtue such as the six paramita practices without concern for one's own life and body. In that way, you should apply yourself to virtuous conduct of body, speech, and mind through the force of faith. Also, even if you have such an intention to engage in practice, if you procrastinate, even though you may wish to practice dharma, your life will pass you by. Since this is taught, not procrastinating even for a moment—as if a snake were in the lap of a timid person, or as if the hair of an attractive woman had caught on fire—immediately cut off the activities of this life. Having given up whatever remains, you should presently and immediately strive for the dharma. If you don't do this, your never-ending activities will be like ripples on water, and an opportunity for practicing dharma will never come.

Omniscient Longchenpa said:

> Worldly activities will not cease until you die.
> Only when you stop will they cease. This is the way of things.[2]

INSATIABLE DILIGENCE

Insatiable diligence is making efforts in virtue, without being satisfied, until you attain enlightenment. Not being satisfied with having accomplished just a little bit of sadhana practice, retreat, virtuous conduct of the three gates, or hearing and contemplating, work to develop your diligence more and more. The sages of the past praised this with a single voice. Moreover, when practicing dharma you should be like a hungry yak eating grass, who eats so that before finishing one mouthful, he looks ahead to the next. Thus, as you are practicing these stages of dharma, resolve to accomplish them. You should remain without even a single moment of your three gates being slothful, at leisure, or without dharma.

Until perfect enlightenment is attained, there are karma and habitual tendencies to be relinquished and there are ever higher qualities to obtain. Therefore, with heartfelt enthusiasm and without being satisfied with what you have already accomplished in the dharma, you should be diligent.

Zilnön Draktsal said:

> Knowing how this busy life appears,
> To practice the genuine dharma of ultimate bliss
> Without being prodded day and night[3] but with the whip of joyful diligence,
> One will certainly go to the land of liberation.

Whether or not you attain the state of buddhahood depends on the three types of diligence.

Rigdzin Jikme Lingpa said:

> A person who doesn't have diligence
> Cannot be protected
> By wisdom, mastery, or strength,
> Just like someone steering a boat
> That has a broken oar.

In that way, the dharma of a person lacking in diligence, regardless of how intelligent they may be, will never be more than the lowest quality. Also, any good qualities a person with no diligence may have are like the fruit of a seed that is scorched: they are without benefit.

As the main method for developing diligence, one should meditate on and develop a genuine sense of impermanence.

The Protector said:

> The root of diligence is based upon the meditation on impermanence.

Potowa said:

For example: Just as one must hit an untamed ox with a strong whip to impel him, you must hit the negative habits of the mind again and again with the whip of impermanence to impel it toward the dharma.

Moreover, Jetsun Milarepa said:

Recalling death repeatedly, one becomes victorious over the mara of laziness.
If you bring impermanence to mind, all that you do will go toward the dharma.

THE FAULTS OF NOT ENGAGING IN DILIGENCE

The *Application of Mindfulness Sutra* states:

The single basis of the afflictions
Is laziness.
Whoever has a bit of laziness
Lacks all dharma.[4]

Without diligence, one comes under the power of laziness and all the benefit of this life and the next will diminish.

THE BENEFITS OF ENGAGING IN DILIGENCE

The *Ornament of the Sutras* states:

Among all the accumulations of virtue, diligence is supreme.
Once one has it, [enlightenment] will be attained.

There are many sayings like this. This is the bodhisattvas' practice of training in the paramita of diligence.

29

THE MEANS OF MEDITATIVE CONCENTRATION

Knowing that through superior insight endowed with
 thorough calm abiding
The mental afflictions are completely subdued,
To meditate with the concentration that perfectly goes
 beyond
The four formless states is the practice of a bodhisattva. (29)

On the basis of excellent, fully authentic calm abiding—the mind placed
one-pointedly on a focal object—the superior insight that realizes emptiness will completely subdue ignorance, the root of samsara, by drawing the
mental afflictions from their root. Knowing this, meditate with concentration that employs the special method of perfectly going beyond mundane
meditative absorptions, such as the four formless states, in which calm abiding is predominant.

The *Letter to a Friend* states:

Without concentration there is also no prajna.[1]

Even if someone has generosity and [the other paramitas], if they do not have
concentration, they will come under the power of utter distraction. Then,
being devoid of any prajna, they will become wounded by the sharp teeth
of the mental afflictions.

The *Entrance to the Way of a Bodhisattva* says:

A person whose mind is distracted
Abides between the sharp teeth of the afflictions.[2]

The meditative concentration that fully subdues all mental afflictions is the mind abiding one-pointedly; this is the fully qualified calm abiding.

This topic consists of (1) the essence; (2) the divisions; (3) the way of meditating; and (4) the result of meditating in this way.

[THE ESSENCE,] PRACTICING THE SAMADHI OF ONE-POINTED MIND

From the *Ratnamegha Sutra*:

The essence of concentration is abiding with a one-pointed mind.

THE DIVISIONS

The *Lankavatara Sutra* states:

The concentrations that are the approach of immature beings,
The concentration that thoroughly discriminates reality,
And the concentration of the tathagatas.

Each of those three is presented in a summarized and an extensive explanation.

Summary of the Three Types of Meditation

The three types of meditative concentration consist of (1) mundane concentrations and (2) transcendent concentrations.

The Concentrations That Are the Approach of Immature Beings

The concentrations that are the approach of immature beings consist of the eight meditative absorptions in which one enters into the non-Buddhist and common Buddhist paths, as well as the mundane paths where the concentration of the formless samadhis in which one's mind stream does not enter the path [to liberation] is like enjoyment.

The Concentrations That Thoroughly Discriminate Reality

The concentrations that thoroughly discriminate reality consist of the nine successive meditative absorptions that are obtained through the transcendent path, or to the concentrations of the respective yanas—the samadhis of the paths of entering, accumulation, and joining[3]—which actualize the path of liberation.

The Virtuous Concentration of the Tathagatas

The virtuous concentration of the tathagatas refers to all the uncontaminated samadhis in the mind streams of the noble ones on the first level (*bhumi*) and above.[4]

The Extensive Explanation of the Three Types of Meditative Concentration

The Mundane Path

The mundane path, the practices that are the approach of immature beings, includes (1) the form practices[5] and (2) the formless practices.

The Form Practices: The form practices include (1) training; (2) the four concentrations of ordinary beings; (3) the preparatory stages for those; and (4) the meditative absorptions that come through the power of that.

These do not have all the factors of enlightenment along with aspiration, and they are the cause of the actualization of samsara. The predominant way of meditating on the mundane paths is with the cognitive aspects of [discriminating] coarser states from more peaceful ones.[6] The mind of desire is regarded as coarse, not peaceful, and as having inferior characteristics.

The first concentration (*dhyana*) is a cause of actualizing samsara. It has the feeling of equanimity and has examination and analysis. The preparatory stage of the first concentration is the mind that joins one with that. When the mind has transcended negativity and craving and has examination, analysis, joy, and bliss, this is what is known as the [actual] first concentration. When this state is free of examination and has only analysis, this is explained to be the special first concentration. As to what is meant by examination and analysis,[7] the *Abhidharmakosha* says:

Examination and analysis are gross and refined [respectively].

Examining whether you abide or do not abide in flawless samadhi is examination. Contemplating the distinctive features of that samadhi is analysis.

In the second concentration, one does not have examination or analysis; one is free of the craving of the first concentration; and joy, inner clarity, and bliss develop. That is the second concentration.

Free from the craving of the second concentration, when there is bliss, equanimity, mindfulness, and attentiveness, that is the third concentration.

The concentration that is free from the craving of the third concentration is a state that is neither bliss or pain.[8] When one has mindfulness and equanimity, that is the fourth concentration.

The preparatory stages for the concentrations are accomplished by [training] in the previous [concentration] as is explained in the *Yogacharabhumi* by Asanga.

The Four Formless Practices: On the basis of attaining the fourth concentration, discriminations of shapes, such as squares and spheres; discriminations of colors, such as white, yellow, red, and green; tactile perceptions, such as Mount Meru, houses, huts, and so on—all three of these [discriminations] cease through one's meditating that all phenomena are like space. Going beyond all discriminations of form, and remaining in a state that is like space, is the formless state called Boundless Space (1).

Abandoning fixation even to mere space [of the first formless state], thinking, "This is space," and abiding in the state of mere consciousness is Boundless Consciousness (2).

Abandoning the fixation on mere consciousness [of the second formless state], and abiding in the state of thinking, "There is nothing whatsoever," is called Nothing Whatsoever (3).

Abandoning also the fixation on that experience of nothingness, one examines the discrimination of the one who thinks, "There is nothing whatsoever," and the movement of discrimination is halted. Abiding in this mere subtle discrimination is the *ayatana*[9] of neither having discrimination nor not having discrimination. This is also called Neither Presence Nor Absence (4).[10]

The eight form and formless meditative absorptions, and the meditative absorption of cessation, these nine, are merely supports for the path of the noble ones. You should know the remedies to the five faults that are hindrances to the attainment of these samadhis, such as the eight perceptions to be relied upon. This may be understood from what is elucidated below.

The Concentrations That Transcend the Mundane

The concentrations that transcend the mundane include (1) the concentration that discriminates reality and (2) the virtuous concentration of the tathagatas.

The Concentration That Discriminates Reality: Abandoning samsara, having the factors of enlightenment, and not having the desire [for higher samsaric states] is the samadhi that discriminates reality.

The *Sutra of Unraveling the Intent* states:

> The Buddha, the perfect teacher, explained, "The pure dharma that I have taught are these [twelve types of] teachings for the bodhisattvas: the sutras, songs, prophecies, verses, special aphorisms, declarations, narratives, Jataka tales, books of extensive scripture, narratives of marvels, and presentations of established instructions. The bodhisattvas hear it well, contemplate it well, train in the recitation of it well, examine it well with their minds, and fully realize it through their insight.
>
> "Having done this, they remain in solitary places; having perfectly settled [their minds], they mentally engage those dharmas in the way they have thus well contemplated them. With whichever of those minds has engaged in contemplation, they continuously mentally engage it inwardly.[11] The pliancy of body and mind that arises from engaging and abiding in it repeatedly is called calm abiding. In this way, the bodhisattvas seek calm abiding."[12]

These are the defining traits of calm abiding.

The [Virtuous] Concentration of the Tathagatas: Again, from that sutra:

The superior insight that integrates calm abiding and superior insight in reliance on that samadhi [described above] is the special concentration of the tathagatas:[13]
> Through that calm abiding, they obtain pliancy of body and mind and abide only in that. Having abandoned mental distractions, they analyze and inwardly contemplate those very dharmas—the focal objects of their samadhi—as images and with determination. Thus, any differentiation, thorough differentiation, examination, analysis, patience, interest, discrimination, view, and examination of the objects that are known with respect to those images—the focal objects of their samadhi—is called superior insight. The bodhisattvas become skillful in superior insight in that way.[14]

Superior insight that is not stabilized with calm abiding is like a butter lamp blown in the wind, and calm abiding that is not connected with superior insight cannot completely cut the web of obscurations. The calm abiding states of the four concentrations and the formless realms are like the peak of samsara: through strong calm abiding, one stops the turbulence of the mind caused by the wind of thoughts.

When one has superior insight, the web of negative views of opponents,[15] such as the view of the transitory collection[16] and the obscuration of ignorance, cannot agitate the mind. Further, it overcomes bad philosophical systems and neutral states of mind. These are the defining characteristics of superior insight.

THE WAY OF MEDITATING

The way of meditating includes (1) cultivating calm abiding; (2) meditation on superior insight; and (3) meditation on calm abiding and superior insight together.

Cultivating Calm Abiding

Cultivating calm abiding includes (1) the support, which is the accumulation of merit, and (2) the actual way of meditating.

The Support, Which Is the Accumulation of Merit

Gyalwa Dromtönpa said:

We cannot accomplish calm abiding based solely on the upade-shas. Even so, should we pursue [meditation] in accord with the upadeshas, if we are disinclined to sustain it, that is the fault of not relying on the accumulation of merit.

First, give rise to revulsion toward samsara. Having looked at that experience of feeling disheartened and disillusioned, then practice. If you do not look in this way, you will never be able to develop stable samadhi because your mind will be agitated by the sense pleasures. In particular, if you do not abandon all the distractions and busyness of daily life and keep to a solitary place, you will not be able to develop concentration in your mind stream. Therefore, you should isolate your mind from thoughts and your body from busyness.

Thus, those with whom you are now connected—assembled family members or loved ones whom you long for, such as spouses—whoever they may be, are phenomena from which, because you have come together, you will be separated. Even these aggregates of flesh and bone that were born together cannot transcend the fate of becoming dust one day. Therefore, this tightly held self fixation, such intense attachment and clinging, is nothing but a cause for the further solidification of confused appearances; it is of the nature of suffering. In particular, sense pleasures and wealth are the source of faults. Even if you have them, you are not satisfied. As your wealth and power grow more and more, your stinginess increases. Because of that, you waste your life accruing, protecting, and augmenting. Ultimately, it will be the sole action that will make you wander in the lower realms.

Nagarjuna said:

Accruing, protecting, and proliferating are exhausting.
Thus, know that wealth is [a source of] boundless ruin.

Accordingly, to be continuously tied to loved ones is of little use. Whatever wealth you may have also has no essence. Subjugating enemies will never come to an end. Taking care of those to whom you are close is also endless.

All distractions, these endless activities, are to be cast away like spit. Keeping resolutely to solitary places is very important.

The sutras state:

Always keeping to deep forests and solitary places,
You will obtain supreme samadhi after a short while.

Even if you isolate your body from worldly activity, if your mind does not become isolated from thoughts, you are no different from an old yak that dwells in the mountains.[17] Therefore, you should examine whichever are the most predominant mental afflictions and discursive thoughts in your mind stream. Consider this to be the antidote.

Further, the antidote to desire is to meditate on repulsiveness. The antidote to aggression is to meditate on loving-kindness. The antidote to ignorance is to meditate on dependent origination. The antidote to jealousy is to meditate on self and other as being equal. The antidote to pride is to meditate on exchanging self and other. If aspects of the different mental afflictions arise together and there are many coarse thoughts, then meditate on the breath.

The *Ornament of the Sutras* states:

The concentration of the bodhisattvas
Is not attached, not attached, not attached . . .[18]

Accordingly, if one abides without attachment toward anything, the mind will be relaxed and strong samadhi will increase.

The Actual Way of Meditating

The actual way of meditating includes (1) conduct of the body and (2) stages in meditation.

Conduct of the Body: Having formed the superior intention—the desire to establish all sentient beings in the heart of enlightenment—you should engage in the seven branches: prostrating to all the buddhas and bodhisattvas of the ten directions, making as many offerings as one can, confessing, and so forth.[19] After that, on a comfortable seat, sit in the vajra posture, or the half-vajra posture,[20] whichever is suitable. The eyes should not be completely open or closed and should gaze toward the tip of the nose. The body should be straight. The shoulders should be neither too high nor too low. The nose and navel should be aligned. The tongue should be placed near the teeth. Not sending the breath in and out agitatedly, forcefully, or with sound, inhale and exhale in a relaxed manner. You should sit, resting within mindfulness.

If you do that, you will obtain the five benefits:[21] pliancy will quickly arise and you will have the ability to remain like that for a long time; you will not be on the common or non-Buddhist paths; others will become faithful; and the buddhas will give their consent.[22] When you have mastery of the mind of calm abiding, whatever virtue you do will grow in strength. Because of that, the higher cognitions, miracles, and so forth, will be easy to accomplish and superior insight will cut the root of samsara. Because you have contemplated these good qualities, faith will arise. From that will come striving in practice; from that, effort; and from that, pliancy; and so forth. It is certain that these will develop robustly.

Stages in Meditation: The stages in meditation are (1) meditating in reliance on an object, (2) meditating in reliance on remedies, and (3) meditating in reliance on the methods of placement.

1. Meditating in Reliance on an Object: When you place your mind one-pointedly on a previously seen image of the Tathagata endowed with blessing and possessing the major and minor marks of a buddha, calm abiding is accomplished. This is called the samadhi of looking at the form of the bodhisattva deity.

Accordingly, the *King of Samadhi Sutra* states:

The lord of the world is beautiful in all ways.
His body is like the color of gold.
All bodhisattvas who place their mind on that object
Will have meditative equipoise.

As a support for holding the mind, visualize an image of the Buddha's form that is as small as possible. Meditate at the level of the image's navel; if you meditate too high, the life-prana[23] will rise up. If you meditate too low, then there will be faults such as the visualization not being clear. The basis of practice for holding the mind with a focal object is mind.

As to the nature of that mind, the *Jewel Mound* states:

If you search for the mind, you will not find it. In that not being able to find anything, nothing is observed. That mind which is not observed does not arise in the past, in the future, or in the present.

In fact, an object either with form or without form is suitable to use as one's object of focus. With all distraction from focusing on external objects being pacified, the complexity of appearances will subside into the nature of the single true reality.[24] That subsiding is not like engaging in the spaced-out dumbness of the cessation of appearances. Therefore, it is naturally peaceful. Since it is not a thing, it is subtle. Since it does not have any characteristics, it is difficult to look at. Overcoming the discrimination that clings to the unceasing appearing objects as being real is the samadhi that is endowed with the complete abandonment of faults.

The *Jewel Mound* states:

Samadhi is the ground of equanimity.
That subtle peace is difficult to observe.
It vanquishes all discriminations.
Therefore, it is called samadhi.

The mind bound in such a state by the ropes of mindfulness, continuously placed on the object, and not being taken away through conditions of discursiveness or dullness—that is calm abiding.

2. **Meditating in Reliance on Remedies:** When engaging in calm abiding like this, you may practice with the help of the eight remedies to be applied that abandon the five faults discordant [with cultivating calm abiding].

The five faults as stated by *Distinguishing the Middle from the Extremes* are (1) laziness, (2) forgetting the oral instructions, (3) dullness, (4) agitation, and (5) not applying and applying. It is maintained that these are the five faults.

The faults to abandon are the laziness of not delighting in practice, which obscures engagement in samadhi; or, even if one delights in it, forgetting the meaning of the instructions on how to meditate; the obscuration of the main practice is, even though one meditates, the meditation comes under the power of dullness and agitation; when dullness and agitation have arisen, not applying the antidote and, even though one has pacified dullness or agitation, continuing to strongly apply the antidote. The eight remedies to apply that abandon those faults are as stated [in *Distinguishing the Middle from the Extremes*]:

The basis; what is based on that;
Cause and the result;
Not forgetting the object;
Noticing agitation and dullness;
Applying oneself fully to abandon these;
And resting once they are pacified.

Laziness is abandoned by engaging in these four: strong intention, striving, faith, and pliancy. The support of striving in meditating on the instructions is strong intention. What is supported by that is the diligence of that striving. The cause of generating that strong intention is faith, and the result of that striving is the three gates becoming pliant and workable. Further, the antidote to forgetting the pith instructions is the mindfulness that does not forget the words and meaning. The antidote to dullness and agitation is being attentive with regard to when thoughts arise and do not arise. When dullness and agitation arise, apply the antidote that causes their relinquishment. When dullness and agitation are pacified, the antidote of equanimity is the antidote whereby one does not engage with force; simply rest your mind without applying [any of the formerly mentioned remedies]. These eight are very important for meditating on the key instructions.

3. **Meditating in Reliance on the Methods of Placement:** One should practice relying on the nine methods of settling the mind, the six strengths, and the four mental engagements.
Lord Maitreya said:

Through the nine methods of placement, calm abiding will become stable. [The Buddha] said: "These are placing the mind on a given object, continuous placement, repeated placement, thorough placement, taming, pacification, thorough pacification, one-pointedness, and even placement."

Focusing the mind on an object, through the power of having heard the instructions, is inward placement. Being able to do that continuously, through the strength of contemplating the meaning of what is heard, is continual placement. With the strength of mindfulness, quickly realizing when one's mind is distracted by something and again bringing it back to the object is repeated placement. Practicing with increased mindfulness entails collecting the mind again and again from being scattered;[25] that is thorough placement. Practicing with the strength of attentiveness—if there is slothfulness, contemplating the qualities of samadhi and uplifting the mind—is the placement called taming. Practicing with the strength of increased attentiveness—if one becomes agitated, being aware of the faults of distraction—is the pacification of disliking samadhi. Practicing with the strength of diligence, one thoroughly pacifies craving, mental pleasure, sleepiness, and so forth through effort. Again practicing with the strength of diligence, if one is able to abide for up to one-third of the day after having exerted oneself to stop dullness and agitation, that is one-pointedness. Practicing with the power of familiarization—being trained so that one's mind is continuously placed and therefore settles naturally and spontaneously without effort—is even placement. These are the nine methods of settling the mind.

Further, among the nine methods of settling the mind, exerting oneself in the first two ways—placing the mind inwardly on an object, and continual placement—by applying the six strengths of hearing, contemplating, mindfulness, attentiveness, diligence, and familiarization, is called concentrated attention. When one engages in the middle five—repeated placement, close placement, taming, pacification, and thorough pacification—dullness and agitation interrupt [the meditation] again and again; that is called intermittent mental engagement. As for the eighth method of settling the mind, one-pointedness, when dullness and agitation do not interrupt the meditation because of one's reliance on exertion, that is called uninterrupted engagement. The even placement of the ninth method of settling the mind, because there is no need for the exertion of continuous mindfulness, is called spontaneous engagement. These are the nine methods of settling the mind.

When engaging in calm-abiding practice, if you do short sessions, you will develop continuity in your meditation, with one samadhi following another. Because of that, you will have the great vital point for quickly accomplishing the abiding aspect of the mind. If you do not proceed in this way and you try to do very long sessions at the beginning, you will feel disheartened. That will become an obstacle to your wishing to engage in the practice again.

If that very inward placement, focusing the mind upon mind at the first stage of settling, develops further, then gradually you will attain the nine stages of settling the mind. During this time the five experiences will arise. When you are on the first level of mental abiding, thoughts follow one right after the other as if falling off a steep mountain. It seems as if there are more thoughts than usual—that is the experience of identifying thoughts. When one is at the second stage of settling the mind, it is like a small river descending in a narrow, steep gorge; sometimes thoughts are pacified and sometimes they are abrupt. This is the experience of resting at ease. During the five stages of settling the mind from the third to the seventh, when there are no adverse conditions the mind abides like the ponds in the three upper lands.[26] If such conditions should arise, wavering thoughts interrupt such abiding. Again, one wards off the distraction by applying the antidote; this is the experience of exhaustion. When on the eighth mental abiding, the mind is like an ocean in which, even though there are a few waves, the depths are undisturbed. Whatever thoughts arise, due to firm mindfulness, subside in their own place. That is the experience called thoughts forming. At the ninth stage of settling the mind, no matter what conditions arise and without the need for antidotes, samadhi cannot be disturbed, like an ocean free of waves. That is called the experience of thoughts not forming. This is approximate calm abiding, but it is not fully authentic calm abiding. In order to have obtained fully calm abiding, one must obtain pliancy. The signs of obtaining pliancy are that one is able to go toward any virtuous focal object of the mind or body. Once the mind is placed there, it will be able to abide there for however long one wishes.

Lord Tsongkhapa said:

Concentration is the king that rules the mind.
If [through concentration] one places [the mind], it remains like the king of mountains.
If one puts it into action, it engages in all objects of virtue.
The mind and body become workable and feel great bliss.

With the mind remaining on an object, without thoughts, the experiences of the pliancy of body and mind—bliss, clarity, and nonthought—will arise and you will deliberately strive for those; your meditation will be imbued with clinging to those meditative experiences. However, after meditating in this way for some time, you will become free from attachment to those experiences. [At that point,] though you do not savor meditative concentration, through attachment to the antidotal aspect of clinging to emptiness[27] you gradually develop and experience the various samadhis of the four mundane concentrations, the formless meditative absorptions, and the meditative absorption of cessation. These are all of the nature of calm abiding.

This is as is said in the *Ornament of the Sutras*:

Let the mind settle inwardly.

And by Lord Atisha:

Supreme samadhi is the unfabricated mind.

Meditation on Superior Insight

Superior insight and calm abiding must be connected because calm abiding alone merely suppresses the mental afflictions temporarily; it does not cause the obscurations to be abandoned. In proper superior insight, the latent tendencies are perfectly overcome through the discriminating prajna in which [calm abiding and superior insight] are of a single mind, a single essence, and function to relinquish the obscurations; it also is imbued with the postmeditation of seeing all phenomena as illusion-like.

The *Ratnamegha Sutra* states:

Calm abiding is one-pointed mind. Superior insight is that which perfectly discriminates.

The *Request of Kashyapa Sutra* states:

What is discrimination? Kashyapa, it is that which discerns selflessness. Kashyapa, it is also that which does not discern that forms are permanent and does not even discern that they are impermanent. This is called the path of the middle where phenomena are discriminated.

Relying on the samadhi of perfect calm abiding, the mind is placed within mind. As to superior insight, after that [placement has occurred], one thoroughly distinguishes the phenomena of knowing what is to be done and not to be done.

The *Ornament of the Sutras* states:

> When one has relied upon perfect abiding,
> Because mind rests within the mind
> And because phenomena are thoroughly discerned,
> It is calm abiding [that is joined] with superior insight.

Calm abiding is the actual samadhi, and superior insight is the aspect of wisdom.

Meditation of Calm Abiding and Superior Insight in Equal Proportion

The meditation of calm abiding together with superior insight perfectly goes beyond the mundane meditative absorptions. Meditating with the concentration of special means—such as the superior insight that puts an end to the extreme of samsara and the great compassion that puts an end to the extreme of nirvana—to practice with calm abiding and superior insight equally is the concentration of virtuous tathagatas. Preceding that, one takes all sentient beings as a focal object and cultivates great compassion. Thoroughly placing the mind in this way is the special feature of all the bodhisattvas. When doing the actual practice, the mind that is thoroughly pacified does not abide in the two extremes; one rests in meditative absorption where the elaborations of subject and object have completely subsided. This is perfectly pure prajna.

The *Request of Akshayamati Sutra* states:

> What is the means of bodhisattvas? What is the full accomplishment of prajna? In meditative equipoise, they thoroughly place the mind on the object, which is great compassion that considers sentient beings; this is the means. The meditative absorption of pacification and thorough pacification is prajna.

When, in this way, one rests with thorough pacification in meditative equipoise and, in postmeditation, one has compassion that is focused on sentient beings, meditation and postmeditation are called "separate" or "different."[28]

Meditation and postmeditation become a single essence when one is in meditative samadhi in all situations. Up to and including the seventh bodhisattva level, meditative equipoise and postmeditation are different. Upward from the seventh level, because they are of one essence, they are not separate.

On the mundane path, the superior insight that is present within meditative equipoise is of the essence of discrimination. However, when the mind stream is joined with personal self-aware wisdom—which happens in the meditative equipoise that directly cognizes true reality with calm abiding and superior insight in equal proportion—one obtains the level of the noble ones that transcends the mundane. In that way, the mind of the past ceases and collapses; the mind of the future does not arise and does not come into being; and the mind of the present, similarly, is extremely difficult to examine. It is without color and devoid of shape. It is like space, not existent as anything. Likewise, it is free from being one or many; it is unborn; when analyzed and investigated, its nature of luminosity and so forth is not found to be existent.

Accordingly, if no [outer] essence whatsoever exists, [the inner] discriminating prajna itself also does not exist. For example, when two pieces of wood are rubbed together, they catch fire, and both pieces of wood burn up and disappear. Once the wood has burned up, the very fire that does the burning also subsides. Likewise, once all generally characterized phenomena[29] are established as nonexistent, neither the prajna that is without appearance nor the luminosity [that appears] is established as having an essence. All conditions that arise such as dullness and agitation are eliminated. All mindfulness and mental engagement are abandoned. Until the robber, or enemy, of conceptualization rises up, you should only rest in that state.

The *Ratnamegha Sutra* says:

> Through the examination of superior insight, one realizes essencelessness. This is the entrance into the state free of characteristics.

The *Abiding of Manjushri Sutra* states:

> Thoughts cause disturbance.
> If one is without thoughts, one is beyond strife.

One who understands that nature
Is called "one who has wisdom."

Thought-free meditative equipoise that is without dullness and agitation, and the superior insight that understands the true nature, is the essence of primordial wisdom. If on top of that one adds the prajna of analysis through reasoning, they will deviate toward the conduct of the spiritually immature. This seems to be extremely profound.

Nagarjuna's *Progressive Stages of Meditation* states:

[Phenomena are like mere sky phenomena][30]
For which there is not the slightest cognition.
Likewise, for the cognition of phenomena,
There is not a single bit of knowing.
Arising and abiding
Appear for ignorant immature beings.

With examination, analysis, and the stains of the mind being completely purified, discriminating prajna experiences all aspects as having a lack of nature. That is why the buddhas and the noble master [Nagarjuna] refer to that as valid cognition.

The Result of the Strength of Familiarization in Terms of the Three Samadhis

Through one's having the samadhi of seeing all relative phenomena as the eight examples of illusion[31] and having perfected the strength of familiarization, all compounded phenomena—and in particular the creator of everything, the aggregate of consciousness, and so forth[32]—are like an illusion without any root; nevertheless, while they do not abide anywhere, one is subject to their experience. This is like magicians creating any magic emanations they desire and having mastery over them and is referred to as the illusion-like samadhi (1). The wisdom of postmeditation of that samadhi is the samadhi that is like the vast deeds of the tathagatas (2). Wherever bodhisattvas who have attained that samadhi go, they pursue dharmas oriented toward enlightenment. That is the samadhi of heroic traversing (3).

As for the unobstructed path[33] that abandons the nine factors to be relinquished on the path of meditation at the level of the Peak of Existence, the *Abhidharmakosha* states:

> The unobstructed path of the ninth level
> Is the vajra-like [samadhi].

From the path of joining up until obtaining the essence of that path,[34] the obscurations are not completely eliminated. Beyond the vajra-like samadhi, all obscurations are destroyed. The vajra-like samadhi, which consists of the unobstructed path, is the end of the continuum.

Thus, meditate in sessions generating effort in samadhi that strives toward liberation. During the breaks, recite the seven-branch prayer, make aspirations, and so forth. At all times in postmeditation, practice the three paramitas that accumulate merit, such as generosity.[35] During meditative equipoise, accomplish the accumulation of wisdom through calm abiding, which is the essence of meditative concentration, and superior insight, which is the essence of prajna. Embracing all such practices with diligence, fully accomplish the samadhi that is endowed with supreme meditative concentration.

The Faults of Not Engaging in Meditative Concentration

The *Lamp for the Path of Awakening* states:

> If one does not accomplish calm abiding,
> One will not accomplish the higher cognitions.[36]
> Likewise, without the power of the higher cognitions,
> One will not be able to work for the benefit of sentient beings.

The Benefits of Concentration

The *Compendium of Training* states:

> Practicing meditative equipoise perfectly,
> "One will gain knowledge," thus the Victor said.

There are many ways of practicing the special samadhis that consist of concentration, which are the main support for accomplishing the qualities of bodhisattvas. Whatever type of meditation you do that is suitable, you should prolong and extend it.

It is not suitable to have an agitated mind that wishes for stability and clarity as soon as you begin meditating. As for those who do wish for that, Lama Shang said:

> Wishing for signs of accomplishment as soon as you start meditating
> Is a foreshadowing of losing [the meditation].

If you wish for signs of accomplishment immediately, your meditation will become discursive. It is a negative sign that you will quickly become dissuaded [from practice]. Therefore, you should not fall prey to this attitude. This is an extremely important point.

Accordingly, if you do not have meditative concentration, you will not see the reality of dharma. Meditating with the samadhi that is without the marks of concepts is the bodhisattva's practice of training in the paramita of meditative concentration.

30

THE WISDOM OF PRAJNA

Without prajna, the five paramitas
Cannot accomplish perfect enlightenment.
Therefore, to meditate on the prajna that is endowed with means
And does not conceive the three spheres is the practice of a
bodhisattva. (30)

If you have not taken hold of the prajna that realizes emptiness, which is like an eye, you will merely practice the five paramitas as the accumulations of a person with vision impairment and will not be able to attain perfect enlightenment. You will not be able to reach the city of omniscience. Having bodhichitta and compassion, the vast aspect of means, and meditating with nonconceptual wisdom that does not conceive the three spheres as truly existent—meditating on something, with someone meditating, and with a way of meditating—is replete with both means and prajna and is the indispensable cause of obtaining omniscience. Thus, meditate with the prajna that realizes emptiness and is endowed with skillful means.

Further, the *Condensed Perfection of Wisdom Sutra* states:

How could ten million people,
Blind and not knowing the path, enter a city?
If you do not have prajna, practicing the five paramitas without eyes
And with no one to lead you, you cannot reach enlightenment.

Without prajna, the five paramitas are like a group of blind people without someone to lead them. Even if they wish to go to a city, they will not be able to.

Likewise, the *Entrance to the Way of a Bodhisattva* states:

All of these branches
The Buddha taught for the sake of prajna.[1]

But you may say, "Then it is fine to have only prajna; what need is there for means such as generosity?" It is not like that.

As the *Lamp for the Path of Awakening* states:

Prajna that is devoid of means
And means that is devoid of prajna—
Both will bind you, it is taught.
Therefore, do not abandon either.

Then, what is it that binds you if you practice means or prajna by itself? Through prajna alone, devoid of means, one falls into the peace of one-sided nirvana and thus does not attain nonabiding nirvana. Through means alone, devoid of prajna, one does not transcend the mundane and so remains bound in samsara. For example, someone wishing to go to a city requires not only eyes with which to see the path but also feet with which to traverse it. In that way, one needs to have both the feet of means and the eyes of prajna together in order to go to the city of nonabiding nirvana.

Further, there are three types of prajna: (1) relative prajna, (2) ultimate prajna, and (3) the prajna of realization.

Mundane [or Relative] Prajna

Mundane prajna refers to the sciences of medicine, logic, poetry, and art. Whatever knowledge one gains from these four sciences is mundane prajna.

Transcendent [or Ultimate] Prajna

Transcendent prajna refers to what is known as the "inner science." Based on the genuine dharma of hearers and solitary realizers, one realizes that the perpetuating aggregates are of the nature of uncleanliness, suffering, impermanence, and selflessness.

PRAJNA OF REALIZATION

Based on the Mahayana, one understands that true reality is naturally empty, birthless, without base, and rootless. Accordingly, one must have all three of the prajnas of hearing, contemplating, and meditating.

Further, when hearing, like a bee collecting nectar from a flower, listen to every word that expresses the dharma and to all the meanings they express without confusing or mistaking them; it is certain that this is necessary to do.

When contemplating, understand the meaning of what is heard. Rather than merely putting the teachings in your mind,[2] like a deer you must keep to mountain retreats, practice, and definitively obtain self-sufficiency as one would smelt, refine, and cut [gold].[3]

When meditating, like planting a *phurba*[4] into a field, let thoughts be without agitation. Cut the extremes of the elaboration of all outer and inner phenomena from within. Freed from signs of what it is or is not, you should see the natural face of the abiding nature. That is the essence or actual paramita of prajna.

The *Condensed Perfection of Wisdom Sutra* states:

> Understanding perfectly that phenomena are without any nature—
> This is the conduct of the supreme paramita of prajna.

Though there are the three root types of prajna as explained above, one should also understand the prajna of realizing the heart essence of reality. For this, there are five necessary points: (1) the refutation of fixating on things as real; (2) the refutation of fixating on things as unreal; (3) the fault of both ways of clinging; (4) the path of liberation; and (5) the nature of liberation, which is nirvana.

Refutation of Fixating on Things as Real

All fixation upon things as real is included within the two types of self. The two types of self are called the self of persons and the self of phenomena. The self of persons is this "I," or the continuity of the perpetuating aggregates with mind, actions, and awareness; or this fluctuation of doing and being aware of all things.

The *Muktakasutra* states:

The continuum [of the five aggregates] is known as the person.
This flickering proliferation is the self.

This self generates the mental afflictions, the mental afflictions generate karma, and karma generates suffering. Therefore, the root of all faults and suffering is the notion of the self.

The self of phenomena consists of clinging to the inner perceiving mind and objects that are externally apprehended as being real because the self of phenomena is what is apprehended as [any phenomenon's] own characteristics.

The *Muktakasutra* states:

The apprehension of characteristics is called "phenomena."

The Selflessness of Persons

Does that which we call the mind or self of persons exist in the body or does it exist in the mind? If [you say that] it exists in the body: this body is of the nature of the four elements, and the four elements are without mind and self; for example, the external four elements, such as water, do not have a self or mind. Then, as for the self existing within the mind, mind is not established as anything at all. Therefore, the nature of these two is unobservable. That being so, since the mind itself is not established as anything, it also cannot be established as being the self.

You may say, "The self or mind exists in names." Names are temporarily affixed to their objects. That being so, since they are not established as being substantially existent, names also do not have a connection with a self. Thus, from the point of view of these three reasons, the mind or self of persons cannot be established.

The Selflessness of Phenomena

If you wonder whether externally apprehended objects are existent, they are not. If knowable entities that are form are divided into their subtlest particles, are those particles [each] singular or are they a multiplicity? If they are singular, do those particles have different sides or not? If they do have different sides, then since they have six parts—east, south, west, north, top, and bottom—you cannot maintain that they are singular. If they cannot be divided, then, necessarily, all entities would have to be of the essence of one particle, yet that is also not the case.

Or you may say that they are a multiplicity. If one particle is existent, then through multiple [particles] coming together, it is suitable to assert that many particles are existent. However, since not even one particle is existent, many are also not existent. Therefore, since subtle particles are not substantially existent, the substantial nature of outer objects is also not existent. These present, directly perceived appearances appear through one's own mind arising as their likeness due to mind being confused.

The *Avatamsaka Sutra* states:

> Listen, children of the victorious ones, these three realms are
> merely mind!

The inner perceiving mind, as mentioned above, is not existent as anything other than the mere label of the momentary mind. Since nobody sees it, it does not truly exist. Since there are no objects, mind does not exist.[5] Accordingly, as to the essence of mind, not even a mere particle exists that can exist as its characteristics such as shape, color, or form. Its existence cannot be seen and cannot be found. Since it is beyond being the object of one's mind, which is what searches for something to be seen, the mind is also not seen or found anywhere through searching.

The *Request of Kashyapa Sutra* states:

> Kashyapa, mind is not inside, nor is it outside. It is also not
> observable in between the two.

And:

> Kashyapa, as for mind, even the buddhas have not observed it, do
> not observe it, and will not observe it.

Tilopa said:

> Kye ho! This is the self-aware wisdom,
> Which is beyond words and not an object of mind.

These verses teach that the inner perceiving mind is not to be found. In this way, fixating on things as real is refuted.

Refutation of Fixating on Things as Unreal

If nothing whatsoever is established as real among the two types of self,[6] you may wonder, "Is it that there is something that is unreal?" There is also nothing that exists as unreal. How is that so? If the mind or the two selves existed previously and then do not exist later, they would be suitable to be unreal. However, since, from the very beginning, the nature of neither a self nor mind can exist, they are beyond the extremes of being real or unreal.

Saraha said:

> One who fixates on things as real is [as dumb] as a cow;
> If you fixate on things as unreal, that is even more foolish.

Expel the view of things being real by meditating on emptiness. However, if you become attached to the view of emptiness, you will be making a "self" of emptiness into emptiness and will turn toward the lower realms. Thus, the latter is a greater fault than the former.[7]

The Faults of Clinging to Both Aspects

Both clinging to existence and clinging to nonexistence have faults because they fall into the two extremes of eternalism and nihilism.

The *Root Verses of the Middle Way* states:

> "Existence" is the view of eternalism.
> "Nonexistence" is the view of nihilism.

Falling into the extremes of eternalism and nihilism is delusion. If one has delusion, there will be no liberation from samsara.

The Path of Liberation

What is it that liberates? The middle way that does not abide in either of the two extremes is what liberates. What is the middle way, going beyond the two extremes, like?

The *Jewel Mound Sutra* states:

> Kashyapa, eternalism is one extreme. Nihilism is the second. The middle of these two extremes is not examinable, is not demonstrable, does not appear, and cannot be cognized. Kashyapa, the middle way is called "perfect discrimination of all phenomena."
>
> Kashyapa, the self is one extreme and selflessness is the second. In the same vein, Kashyapa, samsara is one extreme and nirvana is the second extreme. The middle of these two extremes is not demonstrable, cannot appear, and cannot be cognized. Kashyapa, this is the middle way known as "perfect discrimination of all phenomena."

Thus, even if one does not conceptualize the two extremes and engages in the middle way, the middle way itself does not exist as something permanent. Ultimately, abide beyond mind, free of the cognition that fixates upon even the middle way.

The Nature of Liberation, Which Is the Nature of Nirvana

If none of the phenomena of samsara are established at all as either real or unreal, is nirvana something that is real or unreal? That which is beyond thought or expression, the exhaustion of all mental states of clinging to things as real or unreal, is called nirvana.

The *Precious Garland* says:

> The exhaustion of clinging to things as real
> Or as unreal is called nirvana.

Rahula's Praise of the Mother [Prajnaparamita] states:

> The inconceivable, ineffable prajnaparamita,
> Unborn, unceasing, the essence of space,
> Is the domain of personal self-aware wisdom.
> To the mother of the victorious ones of the three times, I prostrate.

Accordingly, the words that one's mind understands are used from the perspective of conceptual discrimination, but prajna—the nature of one's own mind—is beyond something that could be known or expressed.

Gyalwa Tsongkhapa also said:

> Profound prajna, the eye that observes suchness,
> Is the path of eradicating samsara from the root.
> It is a treasure lode whose qualities are praised in all the scriptures.
> It is proclaimed to be the supreme torch that clears the darkness of
> ignorance.

This prajna that realizes selflessness is the supreme cutter of the root of samsara. In a thousand aeons, even just its name is difficult to hear. Because it is the supreme path that is indispensable for attaining buddhahood, without being satisfied with merely comprehending or merely understanding this nature intellectually, you should make your familiarity with it stable. For example, silver ore has the nature of silver, but until it is smelted, it does not appear as silver. Likewise, from the beginning, all phenomena are of the nature of emptiness and are free from elaborations. Not meditating and not familiarizing will not free one from samsara.

As Shantideva said:

> Without understanding this secret of mind,
> The supreme point of all dharma,
> Even though one wishes to subdue suffering and attain happiness,
> One will uselessly wander in torment.[8]

The sutras state:

> Giving food and drink
> To the many sentient beings
> But dying of hunger myself:
> Dharma that is not meditated upon is like that.

The lord of yogis Milarepa said:

> Seeing food is not enough; it must be eaten.
> Understanding dharma is not enough; you must meditate on it.

If you understand the paramita of prajna in an unmistaken way, solitary places will not become busy and distractions will not arise. Free of meditating with the contrivance of analysis and being free of characteristics; without thinking about existence, nonexistence, or even what is to be adopted or rejected, rest free from effort.

Likewise, Tilopa said:

> Without thinking, without contemplating, without knowing,
> Without meditating, and without examining, rest naturally.

Nagarjuna said:

> Do not conceptualize anything, do not think of anything,
> Do not manipulate; settle naturally and relaxed.
> That nonfabrication is the unborn precious treasury.
> It is the way of all the victorious ones of the three times.

The *Eight Thousand Verses [on Prajnaparamita]* states:

> The meditation of the prajnaparamita
> Is to not meditate on any phenomenon.

The Great One from Uddiyana said:

> As to meditating on the prajnaparamita,
> To know one thing is to be liberated from all.

Lord Atisha said:

> The dharmadhatu is free from elaborations;
> Mind is also free from elaborations.

In that way, meditation on the paramita of prajna is remaining fresh, uncontrived, and perfectly free from all extremes of elaboration.

On the glorious mountain peak of the south,[9] Tilopa asked for advice from glorious Vajrapani, who said, "Rest uncontrived!" Then, as he was leaving, not knowing the meaning of "uncontrived," he turned again to ask. Just as he thought that, he encountered the dakini Shri Dhari, who said, "'Uncontrived' is the mind remaining ordinary, without meditating, and without looking."

Thus, uncontrived meditation is the unmistaken true reality. In post-meditation, you should see everything as an illusion and gather the accumulations of merit, such as generosity, as much as you can.

The *King of Samadhi Sutra* states:

> The illusory forms conjured by magicians—
> Horses, elephants, and chariots—
> Appearances are like that; none of them exist.
> Understand all phenomena to be like that.

The *Conduct of the True Nature* states:

> When one has nonconceptual wisdom,
> The accumulation of merit, too, is uninterrupted.

The Great One from Uddiyana said:

> Realize the nature of great bliss free from activity,
> And through the strength of diligence, strive to accumulate virtue.

Vairochana said:

> Though one may realize deathlessness and birthlessness,
> Conditioned virtue should remain uninterrupted.

Do not neglect the accumulation of the contaminated virtue of body and speech; in the state free from attachment, you should readily take on virtue.

THE FAULTS OF NOT MEDITATING ON THE PARAMITA OF PRAJNA

The faults are just as discussed above; moreover, they are the opposite of all the qualities. In particular, Uddiyana Padmakara said:

> Not realizing your own mind and fabricating your meditation,
> At the time of death, you will go astray into the wrong path.

THE QUALITIES OF SUCH MEDITATION

The *Heart Sutra* states:

All the buddhas that abide in the three times also, because of this profound prajnaparamita, completely and perfectly awaken into unsurpassable, true, complete enlightenment.

The *Sutra That Teaches the Essential Nature* states:

Shariputra, the merit from engaging in samadhi for merely a single finger snap is greater than that of hearing the dharma for a single aeon. Shariputra, that being so, with diligence in the samadhi of suchness, heed this advice! Shariputra, all of the bodhisattvas who were prophesied to become buddhas also only abided in this samadhi.

The *Sutra of the Propagation of Great Realization* states:

Remaining in meditative concentration for a moment
Is greater than the giving of one's life
To the humans of the three realms.

The Lotus King[10] said:

Finding this self-aware wisdom
Is like lighting a lamp in this dark aeon.
It is like waking beings from their sleep,
Utterly destroying the confusion of karma.

Meditating on this will purify obscurations and negative actions. The *Sutra of Purifying the Karmic Obscurations* states:

If you wish to confess something,
Sit straight and look properly.[11]
When you see what is true, you are liberated.
This is the supreme pith of regret.

The *Expanding in the Ten Directions Sutra* states:

> A single torch will illuminate
> Darkness that has lasted a thousand years.
> Through one's understanding the nature of mind,
> A thousand aeons of negative deeds
> Will be purified in an instant.

The Physician of Dakpo [Gampopa] also said:

> If you realize mind's nature to be empty, you do not need hearing or
> contemplation.
> If you understand stainless awareness, you do not need to purify evil
> deeds.

This meditation is replete with the meaning of all mantra. The *Vajra Peak Tantra* states:

> The characteristic of all mantras
> Is that they are the mind of the Buddha;
> They accomplish the essence of the dharma;
> And they are perfectly endowed with dharmata.
> These are the characteristics of mantras, it is taught.

The *Hevajra Tantra* states:

> There is no meditation; there is also no meditator.
> There is no deity; neither are there any mantras.
> Being of the nature without elaborations,
> Deity and mantra abide perfectly.

All hearing, contemplating, and meditation are complete within that. Saraha said:

> Reading is that. Memorizing and meditating are that.
> Keeping the treatises in one's heart is also that.
> There is no view that illustrates it. . . .

It is also said that making offerings and so forth are included within this. The *Tantra of the Secret Amrita King* states:

As for all offerings and *torma*, and so forth,
And all of the various deeds and actions:
Should you discover the suchness of mind,
It is certain that everything will be included within that.

If these are all included within the meditation of the essential nature or wisdom, how are the teachings on the many gradual stages of means to be understood? They are for the sake of guiding those of inferior fortune who are ignorant of the abiding nature.

The *Ornament of the Light of Wisdom Sutra* states:

To understand the connection of causes and conditions
As well as the teachings on engaging the gradual path—
This is taught as means for the ignorant.
For the dharma that is spontaneously present,
What could there be to train in gradually?

Lord Atisha said:

While keeping to the mind of one-pointed equipoise,
Do not make virtues of body and speech the main focus.

Thus, the sign of stable familiarity with prajna is that one will become heedful of virtue; the afflictive emotions will diminish; further, one will have compassion toward sentient beings; one will strive in practice; and, abandoning all distractions, one will not have craving toward this life and will be without attachment. As to the fruition, temporarily, all happiness and goodness will arise and ultimately, unsurpassed enlightenment will be attained. The good qualities are unfathomable. This is the bodhisattva's practice in the training of the paramita of prajna.

31

EXAMINING AND ABANDONING
ONE'S CONFUSION

If you do not examine your own confusion,
You may, under the guise of dharma, do non-dharmic
   things.
Therefore, through continual examination,
To abandon one's confusion is the practice of a bodhisattva. (31)

If those who have entered the Mahayana path do not turn inward and
continually examine their own faults of confusion, they will think, "I'm a
dharma practitioner." Others also may look at that person's outward appearance and think, "They are a dharma practitioner," even though they actually
do not have any of the good qualities that come from learning or discipline
whatsoever. Not only that, even though our own faults are as big as a mountain, we do various non-dharmic activities under the guise of them being
actual dharma. In particular, because of your many faults that are not in
accord with dharma, such as protecting loved ones and subjugating enemies,
you will engage in what is improper. In this world, the fault of disregarding
attentiveness is great. Since that is so, carefully examining the confusion
of the nonvirtue of your three gates at all times, you should immediately
abandon it again and again.

Further, the *Entrance to the Way of a Bodhisattva* states:

Saying, "Why am I doing this now?"
I will examine my own faults.[1]

Accordingly, it is important to abandon one's faults by examining and analyzing them. In particular, if you have entered into the Mahayana, you must examine the confusion of your three gates again and again and abandon it as a means for preventing others from losing faith. If you do not guard against and abandon negative conduct, others will not gain faith. Far from rejoicing, they will entertain various wrong views and forms of deprecation. Because of this, others will go to the lower realms and you yourself will also be at great fault.

The sutras state:

> The loss of faith of ordinary people is to be eliminated through your examining your faults.

Also:

> That through which sentient beings lose faith
> Should be relinquished by your controlling your faults.

Dakpo Rinpoche said:

> Abandon heedless conduct that causes others to lose faith.
> Abandon proclaiming others' faults while hiding your own.

And:

> Not abstaining from negativity even though you are learned in the dharma is a fault in a dharma practitioner. Receiving many instructions but not taming your own mind stream is a fault in a dharma practitioner. Praising yourself and denigrating others through various means is a fault in a dharma practitioner.

Lord Atisha said:

> Do not examine others' faults, examine your own.
> Draw out your own faults like bad blood.

The *Garland of Jewels* states:

Examining your own faults is like having eyes.
Examining the faults of others is like being blind.

Dromtönpa said:

Gouge out your own mistakes by yourself and you are wise.

Accordingly, among everyone's mind streams, our own and others', right now we do not see our own faults that are the size of a mountain; rather, we examine others' faults that are only the size of an atom. While concerned about our own interests, we speak of doing benefit for others and do nothing but accomplish pride in this life. Since we have never examined our own conduct before, we have fallen into self-deception. Taking that as dharma is just like making negativity our practice. Therefore, at all times and in all ways, again and again, examine your own faults and confusion, and abandon them. This is the bodhisattva's practice of abandoning one's own faults after analyzing and examining them.

32

Abandoning Speaking of the Faults
of Bodhisattvas

If, under the power of the afflictive emotions,
I speak of the faults of another bodhisattva, I diminish
    myself.
Therefore, to not point out the faults of those who have
Entered the Mahayana is the practice of a bodhisattva. (32)

Displeased by other bodhisattvas' conduct, some persons who have entered
the Mahayana path speak of the bodhisattvas' faults because of being under
the influence of jealousy and the mental afflictions in general. They themselves become tainted by wrongdoing and, because of that, their practice of
Mahayana path falls into a state of decline. Generally, one should keep silent
about even the subtlest faults of any sentient being, and particularly of those
who have entered the Mahayana.

Also, the *Udanavarga* states:

Do not examine the faults of others
Nor what others do or don't.

It is improper to scrutinize even the slightest bit of confusion in someone
who has entered the Mahayana path, or in any sentient being. One cannot
know the capacity of someone else. Several bodhisattvas took on the ways
of beggars or outcastes: Tilopa was a fisherman; likewise, Saraha was an
arrowsmith; Shavaripa was a hunter; and Vajra Varahi was a leper woman.
The different modes of conduct bodhisattvas adopt is inconceivable.

It is said:

> Most of the siddhis of the Noble Land
> Engaged in the ordinary negative conduct of outcastes
> And did so in a way that was more base than the base ones.

Accordingly, their conduct is beyond being the object of evaluation. The *Request of Kashyapa Sutra* states:

> I have given rise to the outlook of seeing all beings as buddhas. Why is that? Because it is not possible to decipher whether someone's capacity is ripened or not.

For example, a mango fruit has four possible types: the outside is ripe but the inside is unripe; the inside is ripe but the outside is unripe; both the inside and outside are unripe; and both the outside and inside are ripe. In a similar way, with regard to people, some amass great negativity because of being internally mature and externally immature. Since that is so, it is not OK to deprecate or discard them. Doing so would become like an abyss that you do not see or a burning pit that is veiled by ashes. Therefore, you should be heedful accordingly.

Kharakpa said:

> Even though the conduct of the guru who teaches the Mahayana
> May not be pleasing,
> Because you do not know their heart's intention,
> Do not examine the faults of the guru.

The sutras state:

> If you have contempt for a monk,
> Then for one aeon, you will not have the attainment of liberation.

Dromtönpa also said:

> Let go of others' faults, for to do so is virtuous.

The learned and accomplished Karma Chakme said:

A greater negativity than killing a sentient being of the three realms
Is slandering a bodhisattva.
Confess and lay aside the great accumulation of such meaningless
negativity.

Due to anger, not praising a bodhisattva who has given rise to bodhichitta
and saying unpleasant things about them is unvirtuous. You should rely on
virtue, which is the antidote to that.

The Four Negative Dharmas

The four negative dharmas are to deceive gurus and objects of generosity;
to not praise persons of the Mahayana; to deceive sentient beings; and to
generate regret for what is not to be regretted.

The Four Positive Dharmas

The four positive dharmas are to not tell lies knowingly, even at the risk of
one's life; to give rise to the notion of bodhisattvas being teachers and praise
them for their qualities; to abandon deception and abide with altruistic
intentions; and to place all sentient beings, who are to be tamed, in the
virtue of the Mahayana.

Thus, if you go beyond the span of a session[1] without practicing the antidote to the four nonvirtues, bodhichitta will decline. Therefore, apply the
antidote to that, by engaging in the four positive dharmas of beings.

In particular, you may disparage others by arguing about philosophical
systems and through bias toward factions of dharma or persons. Thus, if
you cling to your own system as being superior and others' as inferior,[2] you
will have the grave karma of abandoning the dharma and, due to that, your
virtue will diminish. Not to accumulate even the subtlest karma of disturbing the minds of others is the bodhisattva practice of not speaking of
or examining others' faults.

33

ABANDONING ATTACHMENT TO THE
HOMES OF PATRONS

Due to honor and gain, we fight with each other
And the activities of hearing, contemplating, and
    meditating diminish.
Therefore, to abandon attachment to the homes of
Benefactors and loved ones is the practice of a
    bodhisattva. (33)

We become attached to friends, relatives, benefactors, and so forth, and fighting ensues among those who enter the Mahayana for the sake of honor and gain. Therefore, abandon attachment to the homes of benefactors and loved ones that causes the deeds of the pure dharma—such as hearing, contemplating, and meditating—to decline and be destroyed.

Further, the *Request of Adhyasaya Sutra* states:

Because honor and gain generate desire and attachment, you should examine them! Honor and gain will destroy mindfulness—you should examine that!

This is said many times.

You should examine and analyze whatever faults of attachment to honor and gain you have, whether large or subtle, and rely only on having contentment and little desire.

Shantideva said:

I will strive for the sake of liberation.
I have no need for the bonds of honor and gain.

Lord Atisha said:

That which tightly binds renunciants
Is honor and gain.
That which liberates one from such bondage,
Like a lotus in a fire,
Is an object of wonderment for the wise ones.

Nyugrumpa said:

Think of honor and gain as being a trap or a net.

The Lord Great Bodhisattva said:

Because honor and gain bind you, cut the fetters of desires.

Likewise, Lord Milarepa said:

The dragon's roar is great, but it's just sound-emptiness.
The colors of a rainbow are beautiful, but they will disappear.
The mundane world is delightful, but it is merely a dream.
The pleasure of desirable things is great, but they're the cause of
negativity.

In this way, abandon all craving for honor, gain, or desirable things. Having a mind of contentment is the bodhisattva practice of abandoning attachment to the home of honor and gain.

34

ABANDONING HARSH SPEECH

Harsh words disturb the minds of others
And cause bodhisattva activity to diminish.
Therefore, to abandon harsh words that
Are unpleasant to others is the practice of a bodhisattva. (34)

When you say harsh words to others without examining the faults of your speech, others' minds become disturbed. Moreover, bodhisattva speech—which is spoken gently and appropriately—and excellent activity, such as honest speech, will diminish. This is why harsh speech is a great fault. Since that is so, you should abandon all harsh words, which are unpleasant to others. The *Compendium of Instructions* states:

Bodhisattvas do not use words that harm sentient beings. In the same vein, abandon the many faults of speech, such as speech that is unpleasant, unfriendly, or hurtful. You should speak with words that are always gentle, nice to hear, and pleasant.

The tantras state:

The first thing that bodhisattvas do to benefit beings is use pleasant words.

The *Letter to a Friend* states:

The Conqueror said beings have pleasant speech,
Honest speech, and wrong speech:

Such words are like honey, flowers, and filth, respectively.
Of these three mentioned, abandon the last.

Of the three types of speech that are spoken of here, one should abandon the last and rely on the first two. The pleasing speech that should be used is speech that can elucidate temporary and ultimate qualities and faults and forge relationships. Pleasant, like honey, it is able to bring joy to the mind. Honest speech refers to speech that is gentle and respectable and that is spoken truthfully and straightforwardly. It therefore delights the minds of others and, like a flower, is beautiful and praiseworthy. Wrong speech, which is to be abandoned, is speech that is always the basis for afflictions arising in the mind and, like filth, is spoken in an offensive way in accord with whichever mental affliction is present.

Lord Atisha said:

Wise ones leave far behind words that are displeasing to others.

And:

Free of anger, speak straightforwardly, always with a smile and a mind of loving-kindness.

Kharakpa said:

The poison arrow of harsh speech is of no benefit.
Abandon the negative mind of anger!

Harsh speech disturbs the minds of others. Furthermore, whatever you say, whether it is gentle or harsh, will become harsh speech unless you have the intention solely to be of benefit. Therefore, in the scriptures that teach karma and results, many shortcomings with regard to that are mentioned. Relinquish your harsh speech completely. Speaking softly and in a timely and straightforward way is the bodhisattva practice of abandoning harsh speech.

These four dharmas to be abandoned once one has examined one's own confusion appear in the *Request of Adhyasaya Sutra*, which states:

Maitreya, later, in the last five hundred years of my teachings, when the genuine dharma is on the verge of complete extinction, those who are on the path of bodhisattvas that has these four dharmas will not be degraded or harmed and will be easily liberated. What are the four dharmas? They are examining one's own confusion; not discussing the faults of other people who are on the Mahayana path of bodhisattvas; not being attached to the homes of friends and relatives or the households of those who provide for beggars; and abandoning words that are unpleasing.

Thus it is said.

35

THE TRAININGS FOR ABANDONING THE MENTAL AFFLICTIONS

When the afflictions are habitual, they are hard to cast away
   with antidotes.
Therefore, with mindfulness and attentiveness, wielding the
   weapon of the antidote,
To crush the mental afflictions, such as attachment,
When they first arise is the practice of a bodhisattva. (35)

If one does not rely on the antidote for whichever mental affliction arises—
such as attachment—but rather allows them to arise, such afflictions
become familiar and habitual. Later, countering them with antidotes and
abandoning them becomes extremely difficult. Therefore, someone who has
the attentiveness to examine any situation with regard to the three gates
and the mindfulness that does not forget what to adopt and reject, who
wields the weapon of the antidote with great acuity, should subdue and
abandon the mental afflictions such as attachment when they first arise, or
immediately upon their arising, just as they start to appear.

   Also, the *Ornament of the Sutras* states:

The mental afflictions destroy oneself, destroy sentient beings,
and destroy discipline.

The *Entrance to the Way of a Bodhisattva* states:

These enemies, anger and craving . . . [1]

And:

> ... Toward these, it will be my passion
> To wage my battle, holding a grudge.[2]

Once mental afflictions have been recognized as they just begin to rise up, one should take hold of the enemy and plant the spear of the antidote. If you submit to them when they first arise, they will become more powerful and difficult to abandon. Like someone who is skilled in defeating their enemies, you should become skilled at relying on the antidote to the mental afflictions. If one's sword falls from their hand while engaging in battle, they will quickly be captured. Likewise, if you let go of the antidote, the weapon of mindfulness, you will be plunged into the lower realms. Out of fear of that, you should rely on mindfulness at once. Someone wounded by a poison arrow should immediately pull it out of the wound and cast it away. Similarly, you should stop the mental afflictions as soon as they arise. Just as someone carrying a load of mustard oil should walk carefully, you should pay great heed to the mental afflictions and abandon them. There are many such statements.

Lord Atisha said:

> If the mental afflictions arise, you should remember the antidote.
> If you could defeat your mental afflictions in a verbal argument, what would be the need for dharma?

Dromtönpa said:

> If you go toward the antidote to the mental afflictions, that is dharma. If you do not, then that is not dharma.

This is said many times.

The *Entrance to the Way of a Bodhisattva* says:

> Unless I have the discipline of guarding the mind,
> What use are all the other disciplines?[3]

Dakpo Rinpoche said:

In this degenerate time, reflect on the predominant mental afflictions. This advice is given again and again.

Yeshe Tsogyal said to Padmasambhava:

"Of all the enemies, which one is the greatest?" she asked. He replied, "The mental afflictions."

The Lord Bodhisattva also said:

In postmeditation, learn to tame thoughts of the three poisons
Until all appearances and thoughts arise as the *dharmakaya*.
This is indispensable. Remember this when you need it.
Do not give liberty to confused thoughts, you mani-reciters!

In that way, bodhisattvas engage in the practice of relying on the antidote to the mental afflictions.

36

TRAINING IN ACCOMPLISHING OTHERS' BENEFIT THROUGH MINDFULNESS AND ATTENTIVENESS

In short, in whatever you are doing,
To always, with mindfulness and attentiveness,
Ask yourself, "What is the state of my mind?"
And accomplish the benefit of others is the practice of a
bodhisattva. (36)

To summarize the points of all the previously explained stages of the practice of bodhisattvas: wherever you are and whatever of the four activities you are doing[1]—whatever state of mind you are in, whether virtuous or unvirtuous—examining again and again, never let your mindfulness and attentiveness diminish. With the supreme intention of benefiting others, accomplish the benefit of other sentient beings.

Also, the *Entrance to the Way of a Bodhisattva* states:

Those who desire to keep the trainings,
With utmost heedfulness, should guard the mind.[2]

The *Letter to a Friend* states:

[Mindfulness] is guarding [the mind] with focus.
Through the waning of mindfulness, all dharma will be
destroyed.

Since all of the points concerning what to adopt and reject, whatever there is to be put into practice, depends on mindfulness and attentiveness, you should be heedful and attentive.

The sutras say:

> Whatever genuine dharma one may speak of,
> The root of all of it is heedfulness.

With all bodhisattva conduct embraced by mindfulness and heedfulness, they train in their sphere of activity in a completely pure way.

With all of these trainings embraced by the intention of benefiting others, you should train in the causes of enlightenment for the direct and indirect benefit of others, and not let the aspiration that strives for complete enlightenment for others' benefit diminish. All the trainings of bodhichitta are summarized in the *Sutra of Instructions to the King* and the *Compendium of Instructions:*

> In all activities, train the mind in bodhichitta.
> Bodhichitta should precede [everything].

If one abandons the mind of desiring to obtain buddhahood for the benefit of others, both aspiration and application bodhichitta will be abandoned. Whether or not one is able to actually benefit beings at present, as much as one is able one should not allow the wish to benefit others to diminish.

The *Commentary on Bodhichitta* states:

> Even if you haven't the power to work for the benefit others,
> Always have the intention to do so.
> Those who have such intention
> Will engage in what is meaningful.

Lord Atisha said:

> The supreme quality is the great altruistic mind. The supreme upadesha is to always look at your own mind. The supreme friend is mindfulness and attentiveness.

Dakpo Rinpoche said:

Endowed with heedfulness, attentiveness, and mindfulness, one
must be untainted by all of the faults of the three gates.

And:

Giving rise to supreme bodhichitta, without working for the
benefit of yourself, whatever you do, practice for the benefit of
others.

Also, one should become skillful in subjugating and caring for wild ones to
be tamed in accord with the dharma.
The glorious protector Nagarjuna said:

Evil beings, gold, and drums,
Wild horses, and possessed people:
If you beat them, they will be tamed.

Always give rise to the intention to benefit others. Use various skillful
means, at all times and in all ways, such as when working to tame others.
If one can precede all deeds of body, speech, and mind with bodhichitta,
without being contaminated by self-interest and one's own benefit, then
whatever action is performed will only accomplish benefit for others. Thus,
bodhisattvas practice the training of accomplishing others' benefit with
mindfulness.

37

TRAINING IN DEDICATING VIRTUE TO PERFECT ENLIGHTENMENT

These virtues, accomplished through diligence,
With the wisdom free of the three spheres—
To dedicate them to enlightenment
In order to clear away the suffering of limitless beings is the
practice of a bodhisattva. (37)

All of the foregoing explanations describe the training with effort using the great diligence of joyfully engaging in the practice of the bodhisattvas, and whatever virtue is attained through that. By embracing the wisdom that realizes the lack of true existence and is completely pure of the stains of clinging to the true existence of the three spheres—a dedicator, that which is dedicated, and dedication—all the virtue accumulated by self and others throughout the three times, with none left out, is to be dedicated to perfect enlightenment for the sake of others in order to clear away the suffering of all the limitless masses of beings.

Further, the sutras state:

As all phenomena are conditions,
They depend entirely on one's intention.
Whatever aspiration you make,
You will obtain the result in accord with that aspiration.

Whatever roots of virtue one has accumulated, the result will be obtained accordingly by whomever you dedicate it to. Since this is so, you should dedicate virtue. If you do not dedicate it, such virtue will become exhausted. It will be like an ocean without a single drop of water poured into it; it remains dry. Also, should one dedicate in the wrong way, or in an inferior way to the causes of samsara, or to the cause of mere liberation for only oneself, the result of this will become exhausted. If one dedicates to perfect enlightenment, the root of virtue, it will never be exhausted.

The *Request of Sagaramati Sutra* states:

> Just as drops of water that fall into a great ocean
> Will not be exhausted until that ocean is exhausted,
> Likewise, whatever virtue is dedicated to enlightenment
> Will not be exhausted until enlightenment is obtained.

The *Entrance to the Way of a Bodhisattva* states:

> Whether directly or indirectly, whichever is suitable,
> I will do nothing other than benefit beings.
> Solely for the sake of sentient beings
> I will dedicate everything toward enlightenment.[1]

Even if you accumulate a great ocean of the roots of conditioned virtue, if you do not dedicate that, you will not go on the path of liberation.

Lord Atisha said:

> Even if you strive day and night for virtue with the three gates,
> if you do not know to dedicate it to perfect enlightenment, that
> virtue will only be exhausted through wrong thinking.

You should dedicate the root of virtue accumulated in the three times in order for all sentient beings to attain enlightenment. Accordingly, dedicating perfectly to complete enlightenment is free of all apprehension of characteristics.

The sutras say:

> If you cling to characteristics, that is not dedication. The dedication that is without characteristics is dedication to enlightenment.

Accordingly, when dedicating to complete, perfect enlightenment, one must take hold of the wisdom that does not observe the three spheres. The three spheres are the three objects: the root of virtue that is dedicated; the ones for whom the dedication is made; and the aim, why it is dedicated. The dedication that embraces the wisdom that knows that things are without true existence from their own side, aside from the mere imputation of labels or the three spheres, is the completely pure dedication.

Dromtönpa said:

Dedicate the root of virtue that embraces the lack of observation of the three spheres of any phenomenon to perfect enlightenment for the sake of all sentient beings.

When one has abandoned incorrect ways of dedicating and sees their dedication as the cause for unsurpassable enlightenment, that is the relative dedication. Dedicating in this way while embracing the wisdom that sees things as not truly existent is taught to be the dedication of ultimate reality. However, for the dedication that embraces the wisdom of realizing the lack of true existence, beginners may dedicate thinking, "Just as the buddhas and bodhisattvas who came before dedicated, so too I will dedicate this"; that will qualify as the genuine form of dedication that is free of the three spheres.

The *Sutra of the Three Parts* states:

Just as the buddha bhagavats of the past have dedicated, in that way the buddha bhagavats who have not yet come will dedicate. Just as the buddha bhagavats who abide in the present dedicate, so I too dedicate.

The *King of Aspirations for Excellent Conduct* says:

In accord with the wisdom of the hero Manjushri
And also like that of Samantabhadra,
Following them, so too,
I will perfectly dedicate all of this virtue.

This is the bodhisattvas' practice of dedicating virtue to perfect enlightenment.

Summary

For Whom This Was Composed

Following after the speech of the noble ones
And the meaning of what is said in the sutras, tantras, and
  treatises,
I have put forth these thirty-seven practices of a bodhisattva
For those who wish to practice the bodhisattva path. (C)

The meaning of this treatise is based on the excellent speech that is the Victorious One's sutras and tantras, such as the pitaka of the bodhisattvas. It is also based on the treatises explaining the intentions of those sutras and tantras. Following the perfect teachings of the gurus, such as the noble ones who came before, and in particular the masters who were the children of the Kadampa lineage, the practices of training in accordance with the teachings of the bodhisattvas, numbering thirty-seven, have been collected here. [Ngulchu Tokmé] says that he has written down this text in full for those fortunate ones who wish to train in the bodhisattva path.

Illustrating That the Practices Are without Confusion

Because I am of inferior intellect and little training,
I do not have any poetic verse to please the learned ones.
Yet, because I have relied upon the sutras and the noble
  masters' speech,
I believe these practices of a bodhisattva to be without
  error. (D)

The author says of himself that he was born with low intelligence and that his good qualities developed from training are also meager. Therefore, he offers the wisdom of analytical discernment. Even though he cannot offer grand verses that when recited are able to please scholars who have great training in the scriptures, this presentation is not self-created or false. Through relying on the teachings of the genuine sutras, he has excellently written them down; he believes these bodhisattva practices, or stages in practice, to be without error.

Discarding Arrogance and Requesting Patience

> Nevertheless, because it is difficult for someone like me with
> an inferior mind
> To fathom the vastness of bodhisattva conduct,
> I pray the holy ones will forgive
> All faults, such as contradictions and irrelevancies. (E)

Although he does consider these teachings—the bodhisattva practices just explained—to be unmistaken, alas, because it is hard for someone like him with an inferior intellect to fathom the great, profound, infinite gates of bodhisattva conduct that are vast like a great ocean, he directly asks forgiveness of the ones who follow the right path for any past and future contradictions, irrelevancies, and so forth.

Dedicating the Virtue of Writing for the Sake of Enlightenment

> By the virtue of that, may all beings
> Through the supreme bodhichitta, both ultimate and relative,
> Become like the protector Avalokiteshvara,
> Who does not abide in the extremes of samsara or nirvana. (F)

By the virtue arising from the explanation of these trainings of the victors' heirs, [may all beings through] the wisdom with which all beings directly realize emptiness, the absolute, which is called absolute bodhichitta, and the mind that strives toward complete enlightenment for the sake of others, who elicit great compassion, which is called relative bodhichitta—by the strength of such benefit quickly arising, may beings not abide in the extreme of peace but actually attain perfect enlightenment that does not abide in the two extremes. Through great nonreferential compassion and the conduct of skillful means, may we be equal to the great Avalokiteshvara, the great noble one who is unrivaled in accomplishing the benefit of sentient beings for as long as beings exist.

The Colophon with the Four Excellences

For the benefit of self and other, this was written by Tokmé,
a monk who follows scripture and reasoning, at the
Ngulchu Rinchen cave.

This text of the thirty-seven practices of bodhisattvas was composed so that everyone, self and others, may reach supreme liberation. The author is one whose understanding is unhindered in relation to all areas of scripture and reasoning, the supreme son of the victorious ones, Tokmé Zangpo. The place where it was composed was the Ngulchu Rinchen Cave. This is the colophon replete with the four excellences.

Commentary Author's Colophon

This explanation of *The Thirty-Seven Practices of a Bodhisattva*—the heart essence of Ngulchu Chödzongpa Tokmé Zangpo—called *The Excellent Vase of Nectar* is a textbook that gives an annotated commentary and outline of *The Thirty-Seven Practices of a Bodhisattva* as a basis. For each of the main thirty-seven practices, at the beginning there is a condensed word commentary on the practice's defining characteristics and meaning, followed by quotes from sutras and tantras and then commentary for each of those. This was written down in the manner of explaining scripture by the master Atisha and his heirs, and is based on every single one of those texts, the nectar of the great beings, old and new. Many quotations following one after another is not hugely beneficial; however, to emphasize that all the different schools have the same intention and in order to give rise to certainty and remind renunciants and faithful ones who are equal to me again and again, I placed the blessings of the speech of the noble ones one after another.

In sum:

This excellent vase of the beautiful, precious scriptural explanations
Which was entrusted to me through the essence of the nectar of
    instructions
Is what grants the glory of supreme deathless peace
To the hosts of fortunate beings who desire liberation.

Through the virtue of producing this excellently,
May my mothers enter supreme liberation,
And may they be rich in the glory of engaging and practicing
According to the life examples of the victors' heirs.

May I as well, from this day forward, until the supreme unsurpassable
    state,
Be free of all harmful intentions toward beings.
May I be able to strive only toward cultivating benefit and happiness,
Which is the cause of eliciting the mind of the victors' heirs.

As for the evil beings who pervert the teachings,
May I strive only for their benefit, to repay their harm.
Becoming one who always performs the enlightened activity of the
    victors,
May I be able to engage in the conduct of all the buddhas.

Further, may the activity of the supreme friends of beings and the
    teachings,
The great beings who hold the teachings, increase in the ten directions.
May all beings enjoy great perfect glory
And ultimately be spontaneously liberated into primordial bliss.

Thus, in the sixth month of the Water Rabbit year, while I was explaining
this text, the assembly gathered there requested with a single voice that I
compose from memory a commentary on the quotes and tantras. Because
the one with the roar of the dragon, the supreme, rare, omniscient one of
the residence in Phakdru, again and again requested me to do so, the all-
ignorant Ngawang Tenzin Norbu, with effort, composed this at the palace

of Rongpu Rock at Do-ngak Zungjuk Chöling in the year of the Wood Snake.

May virtue increase!

This printing remains at Do-ngak Zungjuk Chöling at Upper Rongpu Rock.

PART THREE

THE SADHANA

The Swift Path to Awakening:
A Supplementary Practice That Breaks
The Thirty-Seven Practices of a Bodhisattva
into Sessions

COMPOSED BY

Dzatrul Ngawang Tenzin Norbu

Preliminaries

I pay homage in every respect at the feet of the glorious genuine guru, inseparable from the supreme arya, the Great Compassionate One. Please accept me with your great love.

I and all mother sentient beings equal to space go for refuge in the guru,
    the precious Buddha.
We go for refuge in the Buddha, dharma, and sangha.
We go for refuge in the guru, yidam, and dakinis.
We go for refuge in our own mind, clarity-emptiness, the dharmakaya.

Repeat three times.

For the sake of all mother sentient beings, I must attain the precious state
    of genuine, perfect buddhahood.
Therefore, I will practice the profound path of guru and deity yogas.

Repeat three times.

In the sky in front, in the center of oceanic clouds of offerings,
On top of a lion throne made of jewels, a lotus, and moon,
Is the form of Avalokiteshvara, protector of the snow mountains,
The kind root guru in essence.
He has one face and four arms. The upper hands are joined in *anjali*,[1]
The lower right hand holds a crystal mala,
And the lower left hand holds a white lotus.
He is adorned with jewels and wearing garments of silk.
The lords of the five families ornament his crown with limitless light.
In an expanse of light, with the signs and marks, he sits in the vajra
    posture.
Surrounding him is the direct lineage of gurus, yidams,
The buddhas, bodhisattvas, dakinis, and so forth,
And the retinue of protectors with their eyes of wisdom.

With respect, I and the six classes of beings supplicate them.
Supreme protectors, with the eyes of wisdom unobscured,
Through the power of devotion, I invite you,
Along with your fathomless emanations, the form kayas of great love:
Come here to this place of faithful offerings.

Emanating bodies equal in number to the atoms in the universe,
I praise you with speech that proclaims your qualities.
With a mind of respect with pure intention,
I supplicate the glorious guru.

Essence of all the buddhas of the three times,
Your excellent speech is a treasure lode of all the precious genuine
    dharma.
Lord of the gatherings of oceans of all the sangha,
I supplicate the glorious guru.

You who have gained mastery over all the tantras, scriptures, and
    upadeshas,
And have bodhichitta that cherishes others over self,
Lord of all the many learned, pure, noble-hearted ones,
I supplicate the glorious guru.

Your body is pure; it is the mandala of the deity.
Your speech is pure; it is the vajra words of secret mantra.
Your mind is pure; it is the dharmakaya of great bliss.
I supplicate the glorious guru.

Precious guru, glorious bestower² of all that is desired;
Embodiment of the three undeceiving refuges;
Kind lord of wisdom, love, and power, think of me!
I supplicate you; swiftly accept me with your compassion.

Offering:
Beautiful offerings of deathless amrita,
Flowers beautiful to look at, and fragrant incense;
Light, radiant like the sun and moon, scented ointment,
A bounty of food, and music—I offer them to the guru.

The five sense pleasures—pleasing forms, sounds, smells, tastes;
A treasure of all that is wished for, the seven precious divine substances
   and so forth;
All material offerings and those emanated by mind,
Completely filling the sky—I offer them to the guru.

An assembly of ravishing goddesses who bestow undefiled bliss,
Singing songs of delight and a variety of verses of offering and praise,
Presenting them in a great array of ways—all these perfect enjoyments
I offer to the guru.

Further, throughout the unfathomable, boundless realms of the ten
   directions,
All the wealth that is suitable to offer, the vessel and its contents,
Just as in the life example of Samantabhadra
Having excellently emanated with the mind, I offer to the guru.

The virtues and enjoyments of body and speech of self and other
And all mundane and transcendent forms of excellence—
By this offering to the guru deity, may all beings
Enjoy the splendor of pleasing the victors.

Having offered to the guru in this way
For the benefit of sentient beings, I offer all of my bodies.
The great bodhisattvas having fully accepted me,
May all benefit be accomplished just as it is desired.

I confess all nonvirtue I have committed until now
And rejoice in the gatherings of virtue.
I request you to turn the wheel of dharma, vast and profound.
Please remain for an ocean of kalpas without passing into nirvana

By the power of the virtue of self and others shown in this way
Being freed from the bonds of existence and peace,
And the glorious supreme guru having accepted me,
May I attain the supreme siddhi of omniscience.

At this point offer a mandala. Then, the lineage supplication:

Requesting a Host of Blessings: Supplication of the Succession of Gurus of
The Thirty-Seven Practices of a Bodhisattva[3]

E ma ho!
Guide, protector with the ten powers, the victor Shakyamuni;
The bodhisattva Manjushri, Nagarjuna, Asanga, and so forth;
The long lineage of supreme victors' sons of the Noble Land and Tibet,
I supplicate; may the benefit of others be perfected.

A second loving protector of the Land of Snow, Tokmé Zangpo,
Nyakpuwa Sönam Zangpo,[4] Phak Sö, Kunga Gyal,
Kunkhyen Shakya, his heir Kunga Ö,
I supplicate you; may the benefit of others be perfected.

Choklek Dorje, Khyenrab Tenzin Zangpo,[5]
Jampa Ngawang,[6] Tenzin Gyamtso Pal,
Ngawang Rabten, Kangyur Chögyal,
I supplicate you; may the benefit of others be perfected.

Jamyang Gyamtso, Lobsang Döndrup,
Ngawang Drakpa, glorious Könchok Gyaltsen,
Dewe Dorje, and Sönam Drakpa,
I supplicate you; may the benefit of others be perfected.

Pakpa Lobsang, Supreme Orgyen Jikme,
Kunzang Sönam, Dordzin Mani Tsen,
Embodiment of all kind root and lineage gurus,
I supplicate you; may the benefit of others be perfected.

Grant your blessing so that I may extract the essence of this life with its
    freedoms,
So that I may always remain on mountainsides, isolated from busyness,
And so that, fearing death and impermanence,
I may properly rely on the supreme spiritual friend.

May I have renunciation, fear of samsara's sufferings,
And revulsion, with no attachment to the taste of existence or peace.

Grant your blessing that, through this, the fortitude of benefiting others
Through being heedful of positive and negative karmic results will arise.

With the intention of vast loving-kindness and compassion
And the application of the six paramitas,
Having perfected completely pure wisdom,
Grant your blessings that I may be an heir of the victors just like you!

Because the root of blessing is devotion, I, Dzatrul Wagindra[7] wrote this
supplication in reliance on the lineage succession in the manner of requesting a host of blessings.

Then, light radiates from HRIH in the heart center of the guru, the Great
Compassionate One. It strikes those of the retinue surrounding him, and
they also gather into light and dissolve into the principal one. Then visualize
that the principal one, the guru, the Great Compassionate One, moves to
one's crown, and with a smile of pleasure, sits radiantly. Again, think that
oneself and all mother sentient beings supplicate him in a single voice:

Treasury of compassion, supreme noble one, embodiment of all sources of
    refuge—
I supplicate the precious guru.
Undeceiving three jewels—
I supplicate the precious guru.
Embodiment of all yidams, bestower of siddhi—
I supplicate the precious guru.
Lord of all dakinis with unobstructed activity—
I supplicate the precious guru.
Glory of all dharmapalas who clear away obstacles—
I supplicate the precious guru.
Jetsun Vajradhara, embodiment of the four kayas—
I supplicate the precious guru.

Make this supplication three times.

I and all mother sentient beings from beginningless time until now have
wandered in samsara. We who have had to endure many forms of intense

suffering for so long, because we have not considered **the difficulty of obtaining the freedoms and resources**, we are at fault.

Now, guru and deity, please grant your blessings that **the difficulty of obtaining the freedoms and resources** arises in the mind stream of myself and all mother sentient beings.

With this supplication, a stream of the five amritas descends from the body of the guru and enters the bodies and minds of all sentient beings, myself and others. All negativity and obscurations accumulated since beginningless time, and in particular the negativity, obscurations, illness, and döns hindering the arising in our mind streams of the realization of **the difficulty of obtaining the freedoms and resources** are purified. Our bodies become clear and luminous. Life, merit, and all positive qualities increase.

The realization of **the freedoms and resources of great benefit** arises in the mind streams of everyone, myself and others.
Think that.

MAIN PRACTICE

While meditating with the guru at one's crown, reflect on the following:

> **Now we have this great vessel of freedoms and resources, so difficult to obtain.**
> **So that we may liberate ourselves and others from the ocean of samsara,**
> **Day and night, without distraction,**
> **May listening, contemplating, and meditating arise in our mind streams. (1)**

With this supplication, a stream of the five amritas descends from the body of the guru and enters the bodies and minds of all sentient beings, myself and others. All negativity and obscurations accumulated since beginningless time, and in particular the negativity, obscurations, illness, and döns hindering the arising in our mind streams of the realization of **the difficulty of obtaining the freedoms and resources** are purified. Our bodies become clear and luminous. Life, merit, and all positive qualities increase.

The realization of the freedoms and resources of great benefit arises in the mind streams of everyone, myself and others.

CONCLUDING PRACTICE

Meditating with great devotion toward the guru at one's crown:

Embodiment of all the victors, Jetsun[8] guru, think of me.
I supplicate you; please bless my mind stream.

Recite that as much as is suitable.

Supreme refuge, you strive for the benefit of beings.
Please consider me with your great love and compassion.
Fully establishing my body in the state of the form kaya,
Please bestow the supreme and ordinary siddhis.

Your body and my body become one.
Your speech fully merges with my speech.
Your mind mixes with my mind.
Please grant the siddhis of body, speech, and mind.

The guru dissolves into you. [As you visualize] yourself clearly as the Great Compassionate One, light rays radiate from the HRIH in the heart center, striking all sentient beings. Visualize yourself and all sentient beings clearly as the form of the Noble One, with the six syllables circling around a white HRIH on a moon seat in the heart center.

OM MANI PADME HUM

Recite the six syllables as much as you can. Finally, within nonreferentiality:

By this virtue, may I swiftly
Accomplish the lord Avalokiteshvara.
Having done so, may I establish all beings,
Without any left out, in that state.

And:

By this virtue, through the fruits of virtue of the two accumulations of
  myself and others,
In all my lives, may I obtain a support with freedoms,
May I be accepted by a genuine spiritual friend,
And, relying on the excellent path of sutra and mantra, may I attain the
  glorious four kayas.

May there be no obstacles to accomplishing pure intentions,
May all past actions become beneficial for others,
May the guru be pleased with all my conduct,
And, through that, may whatever I do be of benefit to the teachings and
  beings.

The Victor's heirs excellently praise the conduct of awakening.
The minds of those who wish for liberation becoming rich,
May all adverse conditions for practicing the excellent path be pacified,
And may beings equal to the sky enjoy glory.

Presently, may the clouds of compassion of the gurus, yidams,
Dakas, dakinis, and dharmapalas gather,
And with the rain of their blessings having fallen,
May splendor and auspiciousness swirl.

Thus make the link of virtuous aspirations for all contexts, both temporary
and ultimate.

POSTMEDITATION PRACTICE

In postmeditation, look at the commentaries that explain the meaning
of the scriptures on how the freedoms and resources, which are difficult
to obtain, easily disintegrate. Bind the sense gateways with mindfulness
and awareness. Be aware of your portions of food. Do not sleep, but strive
in yoga. When you do lie down to sleep, apply exertion in the yogas that
instruct on what to do at that time; similarly, practice the appropriate yogas
for washing, eating, and so on.

Next:

Jetsun Vajradhara, embodiment of the four kayas,
I supplicate the precious guru.

*Recite everything [from the preliminaries on page 223, "I pay homage. . ."] up
to this point. Then:*
I and all mother sentient beings, from beginningless time until now, have
wandered in samsara. We who have had to endure many forms of intense
suffering for so long, because we have not considered **the need to abandon
one's homeland**, we are at fault.

Now, guru and deity, please grant your blessings that realizing the need to
abandon one's homeland arises in the mind stream of myself and all mother
sentient beings.

With this supplication, a stream of the five amritas descends from the body
of the guru and enters the bodies and minds of all sentient beings, myself
and others. All negativity and obscurations accumulated since beginningless time, and in particular the negativity, obscurations, illness, and döns
hindering the arising in our mind streams of the realization of **the need
to abandon one's homeland** are purified. Our bodies become clear and
luminous. Life, merit, and all positive qualities increase.

The realization of **the need to abandon one's homeland** arises in the mind
streams of everyone, myself and others.
Think that.

> Attachment toward our close ones stirs us up like water.
> Aggression toward our enemies burns us like fire.
> Dark with ignorance, we forget what to adopt or reject.
> May the need to abandon one's homeland arise in our mind
>   streams. (2)

With this supplication, a stream of the five amritas descends from the body
of the guru and enters the bodies and minds of all sentient beings, myself
and others. All negativity and obscurations accumulated since beginningless time, and in particular the negativity, obscurations, illness, and döns
hindering the arising in our mind streams of the realization of **the need**

to abandon one's homeland are purified. Our bodies become clear and luminous. Life, merit, and all positive qualities increase.

The realization of the need to abandon one's homeland arises in the mind streams of everyone, myself and others.

Next:
I and all mother . . . because we have not considered the need to keep to solitary places, we are at fault. . . . When we abandon negative places . . . (3) . . . With this supplication. . . .

I and all mother . . . because we have not considered death and impermanence, we are at fault. . . . We will part from every loved one . . . (4) . . . With this supplication. . . .

I and all mother . . . because we have not considered the need to abandon negative friends, we are at fault. . . . If you spend time with this one . . . (5) . . . With this supplication. . . .

I and all mother . . . because we have not relied on a genuine spiritual friend in thought and deed, we are at fault. . . . If you rely on this one . . . (6) . . . With this supplication. . . .

I and all mother . . . because we have not considered going for refuge in the three jewels, we are at fault. . . . Themselves also bound . . . (7) . . . With that supplication. . . .

Next, the teaching on the path of the three beings has three parts.

I and all mother sentient beings, from beginningless time until now, have wandered in samsara. We who have had to endure many forms of intense suffering for so long, because we have not considered the results of what to adopt and reject—virtue and negativity—and the faults of samsara, [which is the path of] lesser beings, we are at fault.

Now, guru and deity, please grant your blessings that the realization of considering the results of what to adopt and reject—virtue and negativity—

and the faults of samsara [which is the path of] lesser beings arises in the mind stream of myself and all mother sentient beings.

With this supplication, a stream of the five amritas descends from the body of the guru and enters the bodies and minds of all sentient beings, myself and others. All negativity and obscurations accumulated since beginningless time, and in particular the negativity, obscurations, illness, and döns hindering the arising in our mind streams of the realization of considering the results of what to adopt and reject—virtue and negativity—and the faults of samsara [which is the path of] lesser beings are purified. Our bodies become clear and luminous. Life, merit, and all positive qualities increase.

The realization of considering the results of what to adopt and reject—virtue and negativity—and the faults of samsara [which is the path of] lesser beings arises in the mind streams of everyone, myself and others.

Think that.

The Sage taught that the sufferings . . . (8). . . . With this supplication, a stream of the five amritas descends from the body of the guru and enters the bodies and minds of all sentient beings, myself and others. All negativity and obscurations accumulated since beginningless time, and in particular the negativity, obscurations, illness, and döns hindering the arising of the realization in our mind streams of considering the results of what to adopt and reject—virtue and negativity—and the faults of samsara, [which is the path of] lesser beings are purified. Our bodies become clear and luminous. Life, merit, and all positive qualities increase.

The realization of considering the results of what to adopt and reject—virtue and negativity—and the faults of samsara [which is the path of] lesser beings arises in the mind streams of everyone, myself and others.

Next:
I and all mother . . . because we have not considered the need to strive for the state of liberation without attachment to the pleasures of existence, the path of middling beings, we are at fault. . . . The pleasures of the three realms . . . (9) . . . With this supplication. . . .

Next, there are two points: (1) generating the supreme intention of aspiration bodhichitta and (2) generating the supreme intention of application bodhichitta. First:

I and all mother . . . because we have not considered **knowing all sentient beings to be our mother, remembering their kindness, and repaying their kindness, the path of superior beings,** we are at fault. . . . **From beginningless time . . . (10) . . .** With that supplication. . . .

Second, there are two points: (1) generating the supreme intention of relative bodhichitta and (2) generating the supreme intention of ultimate bodhichitta. The first has two: (1) exchanging self and other in meditative equipoise and (2) taking negative conditions to the path in postmeditation.

I and all mother . . . because we have not considered **the bodhichitta of exchanging self and other,** we are at fault. . . . **All suffering, without exception . . . (11) . . .** With that supplication. . . .

Next, there are four: (1) taking unpleasantness to the path, (2) taking hardships to the path, (3) taking destitution and prosperity to the path, and (4) taking anger and attachment to the path. The first has four: (1) taking loss to the path, (2) taking suffering to the path, (3) taking blame to the path, and (4) taking denigration to the path.

I and all mother . . . because we have not **taken loss to the path,** we are at fault. . . . **Even if someone, out of intense desire . . . (12) . . .** With that supplication. . . .

I and all mother . . . because we have not **taken suffering to the path,** we are at fault. . . . **Should someone sever my head . . . (13) . . .** With that supplication. . . .

I and all mother . . . because we have not **taken blame to the path,** we are at fault. . . . **Even if some should proclaim . . . (14) . . .** With that supplication. . . .

I and all mother . . . because we have not **taken denigration to the path,** we are at fault. . . . **Even if several people in the midst . . . (15) . . .** With that supplication. . . .

Next, taking hardship to the path has two: (1) taking kindness repaid with ungratefulness to the path and (2) taking others' contempt to the path.

I and all mother . . . because we have not **taken kindness repaid with ungratefulness by others to the path,** we are at fault. . . . **Even if someone I cared for** . . . (16) . . . With that supplication. . . .

I and all mother . . . because we have not **taken others' contempt to the path,** we are at fault. . . . **Even if someone my equal or lower** . . . (17) . . . With that supplication. . . .

Taking destitution and prosperity to the path has two.

I and all mother . . . because we have not **been able to take destitution to the path,** we are at fault. . . . **Even when I am made destitute** . . . (18) . . . With that supplication. . . .

I and all mother . . . because we have not **been able to take prosperity to the path,** we are at fault. . . . **Even if I become renowned** . . . (19) . . . With that supplication. . . .

Taking attachment and aggression to the path.

I and all mother . . . because we have not **taken objects of aggression to the path,** we are at fault. . . . **If I do not tame the enemy** . . . (20) . . . With that supplication. . . .

I and all mother . . . because we have not **taken objects of attachment to the path,** we are at fault. . . . **The sense pleasures are like salt water** . . . (21) . . . With that supplication. . . .

Next, meditation on ultimate bodhichitta has two: (1) equipoise and (2) postmeditation.

I and all mother . . . because we have not **meditated in equipoise free of elaborations and fixation,** we are at fault. . . . **Whatever appears is one's own mind** . . . (22) . . . With that supplication. . . .

Postmeditation has two: (1) abandoning clinging to objects of attachment as real and (2) abandoning clinging to objects of aggression as real.

I and all mother ... because we have not **abandoned clinging to objects of attachment as real,** we are at fault.... Encountering pleasurable objects... (23)... With that supplication....

I and all mother ... because we have not **abandoned clinging to objects of aggression as real,** we are at fault.... The different kinds of suffering... (24)... With that supplication....

Teachings on the trainings has five: (1) the six paramitas, (2) the four dharmas taught in the sutras, (3) the way to abandon mental afflictions, (4) the way to rely on mindfulness and attentiveness, and (5) dedicating virtue to complete enlightenment.

I and all mother sentient beings from beginningless time until now, have wandered in samsara. We who have had to endure many forms of intense suffering for so long, because we have not **practiced in accord with the paramita of generosity,** we are at fault.

Now, guru and deity, please grant your blessings that the realization of **practicing in accord with the paramita of generosity** arises in the mind stream of myself and all mother sentient beings.

With this supplication, a stream of the five amritas descends from the body of the guru and enters the bodies and minds of all sentient beings, myself and others. All negativity and obscurations accumulated since beginningless time, and in particular the negativity, obscurations, illness, and döns hindering the arising in our mind streams of the realization of **practicing in accord with the paramita of generosity** are purified. Our bodies become clear and luminous. Life, merit, and all positive qualities increase.

The realization of **practicing in accord with the paramita of generosity** arises in the mind streams of everyone, myself and others.

Think that.

Since, if you wish for enlightenment . . . (25) With this supplication, a stream of the five amritas descends from the body of the guru and enters the bodies and minds of all sentient beings, myself and others. All negativity and obscurations accumulated since beginningless time, and in particular the negativity, obscurations, illness, and döns hindering the arising in our mind streams of the realization of **practicing in accord with the paramita of generosity** are purified. Our bodies become clear and luminous. Life, merit, and all positive qualities increase.

The realization of **practicing in accord with the paramita of generosity** arises in the mind streams of everyone, myself and others.

I and all mother . . . because we have not **practiced in accord with the paramita of discipline**, we are at fault. . . . **If, lacking discipline, you do not . . . (26)** . . . With that supplication. . . .

I and all mother . . . because we have not **practiced in accord with the paramita of patience**, we are at fault. . . . **For bodhisattvas who desire . . . (27)** . . . With that supplication. . . .

I and all mother . . . because we have not **practiced in accord with the paramita of diligence**, we are at fault. . . . **Though the hearers and solitary realizers . . . (28)** . . . With that supplication. . . .

I and all mother . . . because we have not **practiced in accord with the paramita of meditative concentration**, we are at fault. . . . **Knowing that through superior insight . . . (29)** . . . With that supplication. . . .

I and all mother . . . because we have not **practiced in accord with the paramita of prajna**, we are at fault. . . . **Without prajna, the five paramitas . . . (30)** . . . With that supplication. . . .

The four dharmas taught in the sutras:

I and all mother . . . because we have not **trained properly in the four dharmas taught in the sutras**, we are at fault. . . . **If you do not examine . . . (31)** . . . **If, under the power of the . . . (32)** . . . **Due to honor and gain . . . (33)** . . . **Harsh words disturb . . . (34)** . . . With that supplication. . . .

Abandoning mental afflictions:
I and all mother ... because we have not **trained in abandoning the mental afflictions,** we are at fault. ... **When the afflictions are habitual ... (35) ...** With that supplication. ...

Training in mindfulness and attentiveness:
I and all mother ... because we have not **trained in accomplishing others' benefit through mindfulness and attentiveness,** we are at fault. ... **In short, in whatever ... (36) ...** With that supplication. ...

Dedication:
I and all mother ... because we have not **dedicated whatever virtue we have done to perfect enlightenment,** we are at fault. ... **These virtues, accomplished through ... (37) ...** With that supplication. ...

Four Concluding Points:

> **Following after the speech ... (c)**
> **Because I am of inferior ... (d)**
> **Nevertheless ... (e)**
> **By the virtue of that ... (f)**

Regarding the session and postmeditation, in the formal session, practice in accord with the stages of preparation, main practice, and conclusion. For postmeditation, strive in activities [that accord with] the commentaries on the intent of scriptures; understand it to be as above. Thus, according to the tradition of the easy path of lamrim, dividing sessions and breaks, this is the tradition of meditating according to the ripening instructions. However, if practiced in the manner of a review meditation, conclude with a fervent supplication.

I and all mother sentient beings, from beginningless time until now, have wandered in samsara. We who have had to endure many forms of intense suffering for so long, because we have not considered **the practices of a bodhisattva,** we are at fault.

Now, guru and deity, please grant your blessings that realization of **the prac-**

tices of a bodhisattva arises in the mind stream of myself and all mother sentient beings.

With this supplication, a stream of the five amritas descends from the body of the guru and enters the bodies and minds of all sentient beings, myself and others. All negativity and obscurations accumulated since beginningless time, and in particular the negativity, obscurations, illness, and döns hindering the arising of the realization in our mind streams of the practices of a bodhisattva are purified. Our bodies become clear and luminous. Life, merit, and all positive qualities increase.

The realization of the practices of a bodhisattva arises in the mind streams of everyone, myself and others.

Think that.

> Now we have this great vessel of freedoms and resources . . .
> May we perfect dedication to enlightenment.

Recite up to that point.

With this supplication, a stream of the five amritas descends from the body of the guru and enters the bodies and minds of all sentient beings, myself and others. All negativity and obscurations accumulated since beginningless time, and in particular the negativity, obscurations, illness, and döns hindering the arising of the realization in our mind streams of the practices of a bodhisattva are purified. Our bodies become clear and luminous. Life, merit, and all positive qualities increase.

The realization of the practices of a bodhisattva arises in the mind streams of everyone, myself and others.

From the preliminaries, the main practice to the concluding stage, it is performed as above. During postmeditation, look at the commentaries on the intent of the scriptures on the practices of a bodhisattva. With mindfulness and attentiveness, bind the sense gateways. Be aware of your portions of food. Do not sleep, but strive in yoga. When you do lie down to sleep, apply exertion in the yogas that instruct on what to do at that time; similarly, practice the appropriate yogas for washing, eating, and so on.

CONCLUDING WORDS

The supreme bodhisattvas of the Noble Land and Tibet who came before,
By the light of the sun of the excellent explanations they gave,
Completely clearing away the darkness of the realm of ignorance,
The teachings of the Victor, a grove of lotuses, newly blossomed.
These days, someone like me wishes to perform the conduct of a
    bodhisattva,
But the clouds of altruism are very slight.
Beings, unfortunate ones, are thrown by the force of the winds of the
    afflictions
And are not capable of gaining the fruition of awakening.
However, with the banner of the winds of faith,
The ship of the swift path to awakening takes one
To the jewel island of definite goodness.
This accumulation is dedicated to the cause of destitute beings' livelihood.

This *Swift Path to Awakening* that is in accord with the ripening instructions of the practices of a bodhisattva was recited in a stream with an altruistic intention for the sake of everyone, self and other. I, Ngawang Tenzin Norbu, spoke this in the Wood Tiger year (1914) called Ananda on the last day of the waxing moon of the ninth month (November 2). It was written at my abode, Do-ngak Chöling.

E ma ho!
Victors of samsara and nirvana, the buddhas of the three times,
Padmakara who obtained the vajrakaya, the rainbow body,
Inseparable with Manjushri, Dorje Tsongkhapa,
I supplicate the Jetsun guru.

With uncontrived revulsion, due to impermanence, arising in my mind
    stream
Training in supreme bodhichitta to purely benefit others,

And actualizing the abiding nature of the authentic view,
With the fruition of the three kayas ripening, may I shake the depths of
samsara.

The prior four lines were spoken by the fifth supreme victor.[9] The following
verse was written by me, Wagindra.

Web of clouds of Do-ngak Chöling Shedrup
Intertwining in the sky of devotion, the rain of scripture and realization
Falls onto the field of those to be tamed, ripening the fruit of liberation.
When that flourishes, may those with bodies be sustained.

Appendix 1

Outline of the Commentary

Corresponding verses of the root text are indicated in brackets [ ].

1. An explanation of the branches of the exposition
   1.1 The way of explanation by the master
   1.2 The way of listening by the student
   1.3 The way of explanation and listening by both the master and student

2. The actual topic of exposition
   2.1 Introduction
       2.1.1 Title of the treatise
       2.1.2 Homage [A] 13
           2.1.2.1 Summary
           2.1.2.2 Extensive explanation
       2.1.3 Promise to compose [B] 16
   2.2 The main body
       2.2.1 Engaging in the preliminaries
           2.2.1.1 Precious human birth [1] 19
           2.2.1.2 Abandoning one's homeland [2] 27
           2.2.1.3 Relying on solitary places [3] 31
           2.2.1.4 Remembering impermanence [4] 33
           2.2.1.5 Abandoning bad friends [5] 39
           2.2.1.6 Relying on good friends [6] 43
           2.2.1.7 Going for refuge [7] 53
       2.2.2 Teachings of the paths of the three types of beings
           2.2.2.1 Lesser beings [8] 59
           2.2.2.2 Middling beings [9] 73

APPENDIX 2

Lineage Chart of the Kadampa Teachings

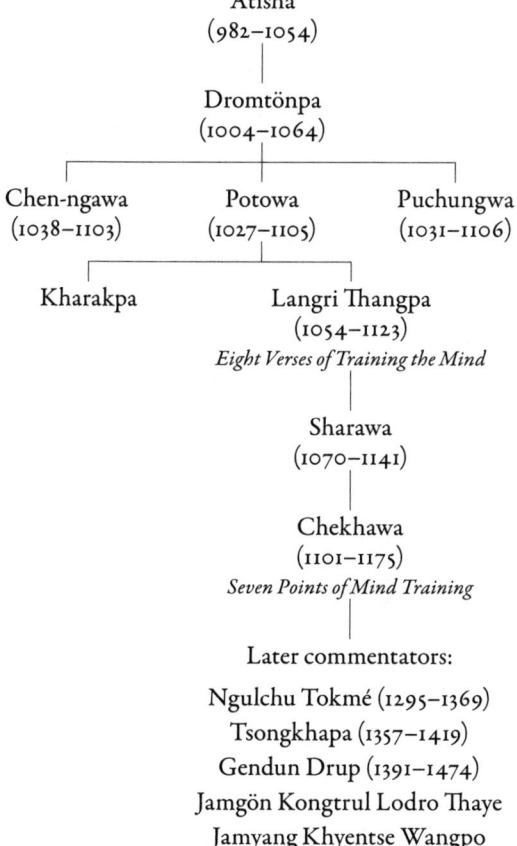

Atisha
(982–1054)

Dromtönpa
(1004–1064)

Chen-ngawa   Potowa   Puchungwa
(1038–1103)   (1027–1105)   (1031–1106)

Kharakpa   Langri Thangpa
(1054–1123)
Eight Verses of Training the Mind

Sharawa
(1070–1141)

Chekhawa
(1101–1175)
Seven Points of Mind Training

Later commentators:

Ngulchu Tokmé (1295–1369)
Tsongkhapa (1357–1419)
Gendun Drup (1391–1474)
Jamgön Kongtrul Lodro Thaye
Jamyang Khyentse Wangpo

NOTES

Translator's Introduction

1. rdza sprul ngag dbang bstan 'dzin nor bu.
2. *rgyal sras lag len so bdun gyi 'grel pa gzhung dang gdams ngag zung 'jug bdud rtsi'i bum bzang* (New Delhi: Library of Tibetan Works and Archives, 2006). Hereafter cited as LTWA.
3. Parts of Ngulchu Tokmé's biography are available in English translation. The introduction of the 2007 publication of Dilgo Khyentse's commentary on *The Thirty-Seven Practices of a Bodhisattva* provides a particularly lucid selection of episodes illustrating this great master's qualities.
4. Tokmé (*thogs med*) also literally means "unobstructed," signifying Ngulchu Tokmé's unobstructed intelligence and wisdom.
5. Revealer of spiritual treasures left by Guru Padmasambhava.
6. mdo sngags zung 'jug chos gling.
7. Wangmo, 165.
8. Ortner, 47 and 180.
9. Tenzing Norgay was born Namgyal Wangdi. Ngawang Tenzin Norbu, who seems to have been his uncle, bestowed Tenzing Norgay's name as a child. (Hansen, 2).
10. Rongpu Monastery is considered to be the highest monastery in the world at 16,330 feet. (Wangmo, 63).
11. Bruce, 45. He also took a photograph of Dzatrul, which serves as the cover image for Sherry Ortner's *High Religion: A Cultural and Political History of Sherpa Buddhism* (Princeton, NJ: Princeton University Press, 1989).
12. Ortner, 133.
13. Aziz, 210–11.
14. *bca' yig.*
15. *shar khum bu steng po che gsang sngags theg mchog chos gling gi bca' yig kun gsal me long*, 458.
16. Here Dzatrul strikes a slightly derisive tone toward the students. The idiomatic expression he uses in Tibetan (*ma dag rgyud 'byams*) implies they acted incorrectly and continued with their mistake without correcting it.
17. Dzatrul, 415–16. Autobiography: *dus mthar chos smra ba'i btsun pa ngag dbang bstan 'dzin nor bu'i rnam thar 'chi med bdud rtsi'i rol mtsho zhes bya ba pod dangpo bzhugs so.*

18. LTWA, iv.

19. LTWA, 422.

20. Translated into English by Heidi Köppl as *Uniting Wisdom and Compassion: Illuminating the Thirty-Seven Practices of a Bodhisattva* (Boston: Wisdom, 2015).

21. *rgyal ba'i sras kyi lag len so bdun thun du bcad nas nyam su len byed lhan thabs byang chub myur lam.*

22. ngag dbang bstan 'dzin nor bu. *rgyal ba'i sras kyi lag len so bdun ma'i 'grel pa gzhung dang gdams ngag zung 'jug bdud rtsi'i bum bzang (rgyal sras lag len 'grel pa).* In ngag dbang bstan 'dzin nor bu'i gsung 'bum. TBRC W29036. 5: 159–400. Kathmandu: Ngagyur Dongak Choling Monastery, 2004.

HOMAGE

1. The five certainties of the sambhogakaya (here termed rupakaya, or form kaya) are the certainties of place, teacher, retinue, teaching, and time.

2. This verse is an homage to Ngulchu Tokmé. His name, Gyalse Tokme Zangpo (*rgyal sras thogs med bzang po*) is embedded within the verse rendered in English as "Bodhisattva Unhindered Excellence," indicated by italics.

3. An *upadesha* (Tib. *man ngag*) is a special type of "key instruction" or "pith instruction" that usually involves some type of person-to-person transmission and is considered to be a most precious and powerful form of spiritual guidance.

INTRODUCTION TO THE COMMENTARY

1. *dngul chu chos rdzong pa.* "The one from the Ngulchu Dharma Hermitage."

2. Lord of the World (*'jig rten dbang phyug*) is an epithet for Avalokiteshvara.

3. *Means* here refers to the first five of the six paramitas: generosity, discipline, patience, diligence, and meditation. The sixth paramita is wisdom.

4. The six limits and four modes are the indispensable keys for unlocking the meaning of the tantras. The six limits are the expedient and provisional meanings, the implied and not implied, and the literal and not literal. The four modes are the literal, general, hidden, and ultimate meanings. This phrase (*tshul ji ltar na mtha' drug dang bzhi'i sgo nas*) is not present in the LTWA edition.

1. PRECIOUS HUMAN BIRTH

1. Chapter 1, verse 4.

2. A similar verse is found in Nagarjuna's *Letter to a Friend*, but the commonly quoted verse is here.

3. *dbus skyes.* Literally, "being born in the center."

4. *las kyi mtha' log.* Literally, "falling into the karmic limit."

5. *Entrance to the Way of a Bodhisattva,* chapter 4, verse 20.

6. *chang.* Chang is a Tibetan alcoholic beverage usually made from rice; it has a pulpy

texture due to remaining unfiltered when consumed. This word can also refer to alcohol more generally, and has been so translated elsewhere in the text.

7. Space, earth, water, wind, fire, and consciousness.

8. *yid bzhin mdzod.* One of the Seven Treasuries of Longchenpa.

9. *rigs chad.* The cut-off class is a class of humans who, although they have the potential to attain enlightenment, as do all sentient beings, are very distant from such a path because of their disposition. For a discussion of the different classes of humans, see also the first chapter of Gampopa's *Jewel Ornament of Liberation.*

10. Mara can be understood as demon.

11. *mi gyo ba.* The text actually gives the Tibetan name of the protector Achalanatha, though based on the context it seems more that likely Akshobhya (*mi 'khrug pa*), whose name has a similar literal meaning, is what was intended here.

2. Abandoning One's Homeland

1. *ma zin pa.*

2. The order of the lines of this passage is slightly different in the *Mi la mgur 'bum.*

3. Relying on Solitary Places

1. *legs par brnyed.* As is explained in the commentary below, this refers to a place where one can obtain alms.

2. Chapter 8, verse 85.

4. Remembering Impermanence

1. When a hair is pulled out of butter, nothing sticks to it. In the same way, when beings die, they leave this life and take nothing with them.

2. Chapter 2, verse 58.

3. *chu shur mig.* A metaphor used to refer to humans.

4. Ones who recite the mantra OM MANI PADME HUM.

5. Abandoning Bad Friends

1. For practitioners who are traveling the bodhisattva path or the path of complete enlightenment, it is important to have a teacher of that path, otherwise one will not be able to attain that result. This is not, however, saying that the teachings of the paths of the hearers and solitary realizers (shravakas and pratyekabuddhas) are not valuable and beneficial in their own right.

2. In multiple instances, the original Tibetan text—which was born amid the cultural norms of early twentieth-century Tibet—refers to women in negative ways: as sources of distraction, as impetuses for improper desire, as persons therefore not to be associated with, and so forth. To be sure, it would not be correct to dismiss such

references as motivated by an unaccepting attitude. One important point of context is that the intended audience for the text consisted mostly of monks; traditionally, some teachings employ negative references to women in order to encourage these young men to turn away from romantic or sexual thoughts as a means to support their vow of celibacy. (Admittedly, this approach also contains the limitation of addressing only heterosexual desires.) However, it is clear that such references to women, if translated word-for-word for a modern audience, could offend many readers. There is a risk that the powerful, inspiring message of the text—developing the heart of altruism with no bias toward anyone—could be eclipsed by the hurt feelings potentially caused by these clearly outdated methods. Therefore, in just this one context, we employ the technique of adaptation rather than word-for-word translation. Negative references to women, wives, and so forth, wherever they appear in the original text, have been replaced by references to "spouses," "romantic partners," "people who are objects of desire," and so on, in a context- and era-appropriate manner. Again, the original intention of the text, in our reading, seems to have been to help practitioners become more aware of the sources of their own minds' distraction, as well as the conditions for the arising of disturbing emotions. Obviously, distraction or affliction can arise with respect to any type of object or person, irrespective of gender or any other category. Furthermore, to be clear, we do not read these references as necessarily condemning sexuality or sexual desire per se. Though not inherently bad, the distraction that ensues from sexual desire is particularly strong if one's mind is not sufficiently tamed.

6. Relying on Good Friends

1. This phrase when spoken colloquially in Tibetan has a connotation of genuine reverence.
2. *ye shes grub pa.*
3. There is no butter to be found in sand, just as there are no qualities of experience or realization in such a person. The same point is made with the simile of a lotus in a fire, which could not exist at all.
4. In the former Indian Buddhist system, a text that someone had written to be distributed had to undergo a thorough review process within the monastic system. Thus, such texts are considered very reliable. So as an indication of their confidence and faith in what was written, at the beginning of their translations, Tibetans would place the Sanskrit title of the original Indian text.

8. Lesser Beings

1. The face of a sheep is long and pointed at one end. The rock here presumably is inverted so that the grinding takes place on the narrower end.
2. *A chu chu* is the interjection Tibetans use to indicate they are cold, equivalent to "brrrr" in English.

3. *btsan rgyal po gzhin 'dre ma mo the'u rang.* Each of these is a class of spirits often referred to in Tibetan dharma literature.

4. To avoid experiencing the hunger and thirst of the hungry ghost realm, one must let go of attachment to this life, which is a relatively small labor compared to the suffering one will have to experience as a being in that state.

5. In our reading of the teachings on this subcategory of sexual misconduct, the explicitly proscribed body parts (in the present case, the mouth and anus) reflect the cultural norms at the time the text was composed. The reader may wish to take a historical view and focus more on the intention behind the rule (i.e., to act in ways that do not violate standards of appropriateness at a particular place and time) rather than the specifics of the culturally informed advice in this paragraph.

6. *gso sbyong.* A time when one is doing self-purification.

7. *mtshams med pa lnga.* Literally, "the five without interval." These acts are considered to be "without interval" because when they are committed, after the current lifetime, one is said to be reborn immediately in one of the hell realms, without traversing the intermediate states (*bar do*). The five actions are patricide, matricide, killing an arhat, creation of a schism in the sangha, and drawing blood from a buddha through a negative intention.

8. The "three supreme ones" refers to the three jewels: the Buddha, dharma, and sangha.

9. *mi gyo ba'i las.* Karma that takes one to the higher realms.

9. MIDDLING BEINGS

1. *zag bcas kyi bde ba.* Literally, "defiled happiness."

2. The desire gods are considered the highest of the six realms and are distinguished from the gods in the form and formless realms.

3. *zag bcas kyi dge ba.* This refers to virtue that is dualistic; the subject perceives a doer, an object, and a deed. Uncontaminated virtue (*zag med kyi dge ba*) is virtue that is beyond the three spheres of doer, deed, and result. Any defiled, or contaminated, virtue is still the cause for samsaric existence.

4. If you eat poison, you will inevitably get sick or die; if you meet a skilled fighter eager to fight you, the outcome will not be good. In the same way, grasping on to composite phenomena, uncontrollably and inevitably, one comes under the sway of impermanence, and so one suffers.

5. Here five classes of beings are referred to rather than the six. In this case, the gods and the jealous gods are included in the same class.

6. There is a slight discrepancy here between the two source texts used; the pecha version reads: *de ldog na sdug bsngal zhi ba'i 'gog pa'am thar pa mngon du bya nus pas na 'gog pa'i bden pa.*

The LTWA version reads: *de bdog nus shing bslog na sdug bsnal zhi ba'i 'gog pa'am thar pa mngon du bya nus pas na 'gog pa'i bden pa.*

•

10. GIVING RISE TO THE SUPREME INTENTION OF BODHICHITTA

1. Chapter 3, verses 23 and 24.
2. Chapter 5, verse 80.
3. The Tibetan word for "loving-kindness" (*byams pa*) carries the meaning of softness or gentleness.
4. This is the Sanskrit word for "suffering" and is transliterated in the Tibetan text.

11. MEDITATION OF EXCHANGING SELF AND OTHERS

1. Chapter 8, verses 129 and 130.
2. Before attaining enlightenment as Prince Siddhartha Gautama, the Buddha, born as a hell being, was forced to pull a chariot with another. But seeing that the task could not be accomplished even with both of them pulling, he took over for the other man with the intent to relieve him. With such a thought of benefiting another, it is said, the Buddha was reborn in a celestial realm, thus starting his path to enlightenment. (*Words of My Perfect Teacher,* 224.)
3. In a previous life of the Buddha, he was born as a male named "Daughter" by his father, who had lost all of his previous sons. When he encountered a man whose brains were being pulverized due to the fully ripened karma of having kicked his mother in the head, Daughter made the aspiration to take on such suffering for himself and for all sentient beings. (For the full story, see *Words of My Perfect Teacher,* 224–26.)

12. TAKING TO THE PATH NOT GETTING WHAT YOU WANT

1. Chapter 6, verse 55.

13. TAKING SUFFERING TO THE PATH

1. Chapter 6, verse 37.
2. In the earlier part of Ngulchu Tokmé's life, along the road near the monastery where he was staying, there was a beggar to whom he daily gave food. One day Ngulchu Tokmé came to the place where the beggar usually sat, but he wasn't there. After a bit of searching, he found the beggar some distance away, hiding behind some bushes. When asked why he had moved, the beggar replied that because of his smell and filthy appearance (his tattered clothes were covered in lice) he had been told by others that he should not stay there. Ngulchu Tokmé, feeling deep compassion for the man, traded his own clothes for the beggar's. Not removing the lice but allowing them to feed on his body, he returned to the monastery. When he arrived, the monks who saw him in such a state urged him to change his clothes, but he refused. Because he cherished all beings and wished to make his life meaningful, he said he would not forsake the lice for whom he had provided a home, even if his life were at stake.

14. TAKING BLAME TO THE PATH

1. Chapter 6, verse 62.

15. TAKING DENIGRATION TO THE PATH

1. Chapter 8, verse 21.
2. Chapter 9, verse 151.

17. TAKING OTHERS' CONTEMPT TO THE PATH

1. Chapter 6, verses 125 (cd) and 129 (cd).
2. *thun.* Traditionally, the day is divided into four or six periods or sessions. Each period lasts three to five hours.

18. TAKING LOSS TO THE PATH

1. *phongs.*
2. *steng gdon. Döns,* "provocations of energy in the sense of disturbances tied to the individual's psychoenergetic dimension, refers both to the classes of beings that cause disturbances and the disturbances themselves, which are doubting, and imply the process of the formation of doubt as well, negative provocations, provocations of negative energy, energy-provocations." (Jim Valby.) The döns mentioned here are a particular class called the planetary döns.
3. Snow and rain are typically considered adverse conditions, but this adage shows that difficulties can be beneficial.
4. When beings realize the nature of reality, all phenomena, which are mere appearances, become mere shifting events within the dharmata, or basic reality.

19. TAKING GAIN TO THE PATH

1. Vaishravana is the god of wealth.

20. TAKING OBJECTS OF AGGRESSION TO THE PATH

1. *Entrance to the Way of a Bodhisattva,* chapter 5, verse 12.
2. Potowa, Chen-ngawa, and Puchungwa were the three principal disciples of the Kadampa master Dromtönpa. They are often referred to as the Three Brothers (*sku mched gsum*).
3. Asanga, after diligently doing the practice of Maitreya for twelve years, finally left his retreat, discouraged that he had not yet had a vision of Maitreya. On his way into the town, along the road he saw a dog who was badly wounded, with maggots growing inside the wound. Feeling great compassion for the dog, Asanga decided he

should help her by first removing all of the maggots that were tormenting her. So as not to kill the maggots in the process, he decided he could use his tongue to safely relocate them. Asanga closed his eyes and bent over to begin the task when suddenly the dog transformed and appeared as Maitreya. Asanga asked, "Why have you taken so long to come to me?" Maitreya answered, "I was with you all along, but because you had not generated the merit necessary to see me, I remained hidden. Because of this great compassion you have shown, you can now see me." See also *The Words of My Perfect Teacher.*

21. TAKING OBJECTS OF ATTACHMENT TO THE PATH

1. *rnag thog bcags 'khel.* Literally, "to bring the scalpel right down on the infection."
2. The Buddha.
3. The vows of self-liberation, which include the precepts of novice monks and nuns, fully ordained monks and nuns, and laypeople.
4. Mantrayana is an alternative name for the tantric path, a special path within the Mahayana school that uses methods such as deity visualization and mantra recitation to help the practitioner accomplish enlightenment for the benefit of all sentient beings. The Mantrayana is said to help practitioners reach the goals of liberation and enlightenment more swiftly than by relying on the common methods of the Mahayana path in general.
5. *ganachakra.*
6. The Tibetan translation of the Sanskrit word *amrita* (*bdud brtsi*) is composed of two Tibetan words; rendered literally into English, it means "demon elixir." The passage below gives an etymological interpretation of the Tibetan word.
7. *jnanasattva.*
8. Dharanis, such as the hundred-syllable mantra of Vajrasattva, are often said as blessings or function as a means of purification.
9. *Entrance to the Way of a Bodhisattva*, chapter 6, verse 123.
10. Angulimala (Finger-Garlanded One) had a close relationship with his own guru's wife. Out of jealousy and as a plot to get Angulimala killed, the guru incited him to kill one thousand men as a mandatory offering to him.
11. Queen Tsepongza, wife of King Trisong Detsen, maintained airs of devotion and respect toward Vairochana while secretly plotting with evil ministers to have him exiled.
12. *yar than pa brgyas mi 'drongs mar then gcig gis drangs.* Creating a habit of strong virtue is very difficult, but falling into negative, destructive behavior is very easy.
13. Nagpopa, also known as Kanha or Krishnacharya, was one of the eighty-four mahasiddhas of India. Asked by a female tantric master to carry something back to his main guru, he was told not to open the package until he reached his master to give it to him. Out of curiosity, he disobeyed and opened the package, which contained ritual ornaments. He then put them on and, gaining supernatural abilities, indulged

in their use. Because of his pride and disregard of the master's instructions, it is said, he was not able to attain complete enlightenment in that lifetime.

14. This is in contrast to a blessing abhisheka, which lamas give frequently without requiring the students to keep any particular commitments. At the time a true abhisheka is bestowed, however, the students take on samaya vows, in which they commit to work continuously with the practice for which they received the abhisheka.

15. It is said that the colors of a peacock's feathers become more vivid and bright when it eats poison.

16. Gampopa.

22. MEDITATIVE EQUIPOISE FREE FROM CLINGING TO ELABORATIONS

1. *ci'i ngo bor ma grub.*
2. Padmasambhava to Yeshe Tsogyal.

24. ABANDONING TAKING OBJECTS OF AVERSION AS TRULY EXISTENT

1. In order to attain the bodhisattva levels, one must have enough of the two accumulations of merit and wisdom. If one holds things to be truly existent, one will never have enough accumulation.

25. THE MEANS OF GENEROSITY

1. *gzhan yang 'jug pa las.* Translated here as "Entrance," *'jug pa* seems to refer to either the *Entrance to the Way of a Bodhisattva* (*spyod 'jug*) or *Entrance to the Middle Way* (*dbu ma 'jug pa*); however, this exact quotation (*gtong ba sbyin pa'i pha rol phyin*) was not found in either of those texts.

2. Also known as the *Sutra of the Three Heaps*, it is often used in confession practices.

3. The Tibetan gives another name (*rgyal bu snying stobs chen po*), but Mahasattva (*sems dpa' chen po*) is how the prince is referred to in the Jataka tales.

4. When the son of the Indian king Surabhibhadra asked Nagarjuna to cut off his head so that he could inherit his father's kingdom, Nagarjuna willingly offered it. However, when the prince tried to cut it off with his sword, he was not able to; it was like cutting thin air. Nagarjuna said that because he had purified the maturing karmic effects of having used weapons in the past, using them on him would be of no avail. However, because he had once killed an insect while cutting a blade of kusha grass, he told the prince that if he found a blade of kusha grass to use, he would be able to cut off his head. The prince did so and was successful. Nagarjuna then entered nirvana saying that he would return to that very body in the future. (*Words of My Perfect Teacher*, 122.)

5. Potowa, Puchungwa, and Chen-ngawa.

6. Atisha.

7. "Heat" is the first of the "four aspects of ascertainment" on the path of joining.

8. In traditional shrine rooms there is often a large single butter lamp that has a large wick and a great store of butter as fuel for the flame, allowing it to burn for many days without replenishing.

9. That is, until you attain the wisdom of selflessness.

10. *dkar phyogs rnams.* The "pure ones" refers to the gods and other sublime beings. The quote indicates that one does not need to be able to benefit others directly, but if one simply recites sutras, prayers, and so forth, the sublime beings will listen and act for the benefit of others.

11. Virtues that are performed on the relative level, where one still perceives the three spheres: doer, deed, and result (or beneficiary).

26. The Means of Discipline

1. The seven types of pratimoksha vows are those of fully ordained monks and nuns, novice monks and nuns, probationary nuns, and male and female laypeople.

2. *yum.*

3. *tshang pa'i 'jig rten.* The realms of the god Brahma, which are the form realms. Although they are still within samsaric existence, it is taught that one must have accumulated great merit through discipline to take birth in these states, which are free of all the sufferings of the six levels of the desire realm.

4. Literally, "steering the mind" (*sems bsgyur*).

5. The Tibetan text indicates eleven points, but there appear to be twelve.

6. *dam pa gsum.* Any activity in the Mahayana system should be done in three phases: in the beginning, one should give rise to bodhichitta; in the middle, the actual practice should be done without conceptualization; and at the end, one should dedicate the merit of the activity to all sentient beings' attainment of buddhahood.

7. The Lord of Death.

27. The Means of Patience

1. Chapter 6, verse 1.

2. *Entrance to the Way of a Bodhisattva,* chapter 6 verse 2.

3. *ko long gtsang btsan pas dam par 'dugs pa 'di* (obscure passage).

4. *bdud bsgrub pa yin.* Maras are a personification of obstacles or harmful conditions.

5. *sprang.* Literally, beggar, poor, or lowly one.

6. Literally, "aim your death at an empty cave" (*shi phugs brag stong la gtad*).

7. Due to great accumulations of merit, someone who is a chakravartin king will naturally amass subjects and a dominion over which to rule. The Buddha, at his birth, was prophesied to become either a chakravartin king or a great spiritual being. Due to his revulsion with worldly pleasures and activities, he forsook his life as a ruler and began spiritual practice.

8. The *Eight Great Words of Wonder* and the *Twelve Vajra Laughs* are teachings given in the context of the Great Perfection, or Dzogchen, considered to be the highest view and practice in the Nyingma tradition.
9. Chapter 6, verse 6 (cd).

28. The Means of Diligence

1. *Entrance to the Way of a Bodhisattva,* chapter 7, verse 2.
2. *nam zhag dus na zin pa chos nyid yin.*
3. If one has genuine diligence or enthusiasm oneself and does not have to be urged or pushed along each step of the way by someone else, then one will definitely attain enlightenment.
4. *nyon mongs kyi gzhi gcig ni// le lo yin de gang la yod// gang la le lo gcig yod pa// de la chos kun med pa yin//*

29. The Means of Meditative Concentration

1. The word *samten* (*bsam gtan*) in Tibetan literally means "stable mind." When translating texts from Sanskrit, the Tibetan translators most often used this word to translate *dhyana,* which is the name of the fifth paramita. In other works, this word has been translated into English as "meditation," "meditative concentration," and just "concentration." I have used the latter two terms interchangeably for *samten* and reserved "meditation" for the Tibetan *gom* (*sgom*).
2. Chapter 8, verse 1(cd). From this point onward, the LTWA edition and the source text used for this translation differ markedly. The LTWA edition's section on meditative concentration (*bsam gtan*) is much shorter.
3. The paths of accumulation and joining are the first two of what are known as the five paths. These five paths all the stages from embarking on the path all the way up to complete enlightenment. The remaining three (not directly mentioned in this passage) are the paths of seeing, meditation, and no more learning. These three are included under what is referred to below as the virtuous concentration of the tathagatas. The path of "entering" refers to the moment one begins practicing on the path of accumulation.
4. The path of seeing and the first bhumi, or level, coincide with each other. This is the point when emptiness is directly realized. The subsequent levels are stages in the development of stability.
5. The Buddhist Abhidharma literature teaches that there are three realms within samsara: the desire realm, which includes the six types of beings (animals, humans, gods, etc.), and the form and formless realms. It is possible to take rebirth in any of these realms. The beings of the desire realm have very little meditative stability; those in the form realm have a great deal of stability; and the meditation of the formless-realm beings is so deep that they do not even perceive coarse forms. The form and formless realms may also be accessed via meditative concentration while one has the

support (or body) of a human or god of the desire realm. Here the Tibetan, instead of *zug kham* (*gzugs khams*) which would be translated as "form realm," has *zug chö* (*gzugs spyod*), with *chö* meaning "conduct" or, here, "practice." Thus, the emphasis here is on the mind state rather than on an ontological plane of existence.

6. When progressing on the mundane paths, one analyzes the coarseness of the level on which one is currently meditating in comparison to the subtleness of the next higher level. For example, someone in the first concentration would investigate the coarse aspects of that in comparison to the second concentration.

7. *rtog pa dang dpyod pa.*

8. This state free of bliss or pain the Buddha taught to be an even subtler form of happiness, more sublime than "bliss."

9. This is different from the twelve ayatanas of the sense perceptions and their objects. Here each of the formless states is individually referred to as an ayatana.

10. This formless state is also referred to as the Peak of Existence.

11. *sems gang gis yid la byed pa'i sems de nang du rgyun chags su yid la byed do.*

12. See also Powers, *Wisdom of Buddha,* 151.

13. From the beginning of the quote up to here is not found together with what follows in at least some versions of the original sutra.

14. See also Powers, 151.

15. In the context of debate, the role of the opponent is to hold a root thesis, and the challenger's task is to refute that thesis. In older Buddhist literature, this "opponent" is often someone who is not a Buddhist or holds the position of a lower philosophical system.

16. The view of the transitory collection (*'jig tshogs*) is the view that holds the five aggregates, which are impermanent and not singular, to be a single and permanent self.

17. If you stay in solitary places, but your mind is distracted, just like a yak's, it will not accomplish any benefit.

18. Chapter 16, verse 34. This quotation, in the context of where it is found in the *Ornament of the Sutras,* refers to the various types of attachment that are resistant tendencies toward fully actualizing the paramitas. The repetition demonstrates that bodhisattvas are *not* attached in each case. For each paramita there are seven types of attachment; however, Ngawang Tenzin Norbu did not use the entire verse when he set this quotation, and so "not attached" is only written three times here (Thurman 204).

19. The seven branches are prostrating, offering, confession, rejoicing, requesting to teach, requesting to remain and not pass into nirvana, and dedication.

20. Half-vajra posture (*skyil krung phyed*) is with one leg placed in front of the other directly on the floor. It is sometimes called the heroic posture (*sems dpa'i skyil krung*).

21. *rgyu mtshan lnga.*

22. The buddhas will give their consent for your progressing on the path, attaining enlightenment, and so forth.

23. *srog rlung.* An illness in which the prana, or energetic wind, gets stuck in the heart center.

24. *chos nyid, dharmata.*

25. *sems rgya chen po las yang yang bsdus.*

26. *lung pa phu gsum.* Presumably the "three upper lands" was a place in or near Tibet where the author knew there to be very still waters.

27. Clinging to emptiness is the antidote for clinging to true existence. If one maintains attachment to that, one will develop the four mundane concentrations but not the transcendent concentrations.

28. When the meditation session and the postmeditation period, when one is not formally meditating, are seen as separate, there is no continuity of samadhi.

29. Generally characterized phenomena are those objects that are established only through concepts, and so they exist merely as concepts and not substantially. This is in contrast to specifically characterized phenomena, which are defined as that which is "not merely named by thought, it is actually existent" (*rtog pas btags tsam ma yin par rang dngos nas grub pa*).

30. The first line of this quotation, although it does not appear in the commentary, has been provided to indicate what is referred to by the relative pronoun in the following line. This comes from verses 9 and 10 in Nagarjuna's text. "Sky phenomena" refers to things that have no substantial existence, such as a sky flower. Because they are nonexistent, they cannot be cognized.

31. *sgyu ma'i dpe brgyad.* The eight examples of the illusion-like nature of all phenomena are a dream, a magical illusion, a hallucination, a mirage, an echo, a city of gandharvas, a reflection, and an apparition.

32. The aggregate of consciousness perceives entities (both internal and external) without conceptions or labels. It is "raw perception," so to speak. Based on the aggregate of consciousness, also called "the primary mind," the other aggregates of mind arise. These consist of the mind's tendencies to label things, the mental afflictions, virtuous mind states, and so on. Here the aggregate of consciousness is called the creator of everything, because it is the basis of our experience.

33. "Unobstructed path" (*bar chad med lam*) is a term used in the abhidharma to refer to a stage of the path where obscurations are in the process of being relinquished. There are many unobstructed paths that one encounters along the overall path to enlightenment; the last of those is the vajra-like samadhi described here. Having entered it, one remains on an unobstructed path until all of its factors to be abandoned have been abandoned. At that point, one enters its respective path of liberation. This process is somewhat complicated in its description and is discussed in detail in the sixth chapter of the *Abhidharmakosha.*

34. "That path" refers to the unobstructed path which is the vajra-like samadhi.

35. The three paramitas of the accumulation of merit are generosity, discipline, and patience.

36. *mngon shes.* Often translated as "clairvoyance" but including all the supernormal abilities that arise due to deep samadhi.

30. The Wisdom of Prajna

1. Chapter 9, verse 1.
2. *bsam pa'i dus su thos pa'i don shes blo dang yin blo tsam du ma bzhag par.*
3. This is the traditional simile for how to examine the Buddha's teachings, as advised by the Buddha himself.
4. A *phurba* is a dagger-like ritual implement.
5. One way of defining *mind* is to say it is that which apprehends objects. Each moment of cognition is dependent on there being an object that is cognized. If there is no object that can exist, likewise, an apprehender of objects cannot exist.
6. The self of persons and the self of phenomena.
7. That is, fixating on emptiness as real is a greater fault than fixating on things as real: If one clings to emptiness as being real, then one falls into the danger of disregarding karma, cause and effect, and may be inclined to engage in unvirtuous actions, mistakenly considering such actions to be merely "empty." This would then become the cause of rebirth in the lower realms.
8. *Entrance to the Way of a Bodhisattva,* chapter 5, verse 17.
9. This could refer to Shri Parvata in Sri Lanka.
10. One of the manifestations of Guru Padmasambhava.
11. *yang dag blta.*

31. Examining and Abandoning One's Confusion

1. Chapter 8, verse 161 (cd).

32. Abandoning Speaking of the Faults of Bodhisattvas

1. Practitioners divide the day into four or more meditation and postmeditation sessions so that one is always involved in dharma practice of some type.
2. Literally, "cling to your own system as being divine (*lhar blta*) and others as demonic (*'dre lta bur*)."

35. The Trainings for Abandoning the Mental Afflictions

1. Chapter 4, verse 28.
2. Chapter 4, verse 43 (ab).
3. Chapter 5, verse 18 (cd).

36. Training in Accomplishing Others' Benefit through Mindfulness and Attentiveness

1. The four activities are walking, moving, sitting, and lying down.
2. Chapter 5, verse 1.

37. Training in Dedicating Virtue to Perfect Enlightenment

1. Chapter 5, verse 101.

The Sadhana

1. Anjali is a gesture of homage and offering in which the palms of the hands are joined at the level of the heart with fingers pointed upward.
2. *dpal ster.* An epithet for Vaishravana, the god of wealth.
3. This lineage supplication, also by Ngawang Tenzin Norbu, was composed separately and has been inserted here.
4. *gnyag phub sod bzang* (1341–1433). Studied at Sakya Monastery and the Kadampa monasteries of Sangpu and Tsetang.
5. *mkhyen rab bstan 'dzin bzang.* The Seventh Chöje Trichen.
6. *mkhyen rab byams pa ngag dbang lhun grub.* The Ninth Chöje Trichen.
7. Wagindra means "Ngawang" (*ngag dbang*), or Lord of Speech.
8. Jetsun is an honorific term that could roughly be rendered as "honorable one."
9. The Fifth Dalai Lama.

SELECTED BIBLIOGRAPHY

Bruce, Charles Granville. *The Assault on Mount Everest, 1922*. Varanasi: Pilgrims Publishing, 2002.

Dragpa, Chökyi. *Uniting Wisdom and Compassion: Illuminating the Thirty-Seven Practices of a Bodhisattva*. Translated by Heidi I. Köppl. Boston: Wisdom, 2004.

Dzatrul, Ngawang Tenzin Norbu. *Rgyal sras lag len so bdun gyi 'grel pa gzhung dang gdams zung 'jug bdud rtsi 'i bum bzang*. Publisher's preface. Dharamsala: Library of Tibetan Works and Archives, 2006.

Hansen, Peter H. "Tenzing Norgay [*known as* Sherpa Tenzing] (1914–1986), mountaineer." In *Oxford Dictionary of National Biography*. January 6, 2011. Accessed August 15, 2018. https://doi.org/10.1093/ref:odnb/50064.

Khyentse, Dilgo. *The Heart of Compassion: The Thirty-Seven Verses on the Practice of a Bodhisattva*. Translated by the Padmakara Translation Group. Boston: Shambhala, 2007.

Ortner, Sherry B. *High Religion: A Cultural and Political History of Sherpa Buddhism*. Princeton, NJ: Princeton University Press, 1989.

Palmo, Ani Jinpa, trans. *The Great Image: The Life Story of Vairochana the Translator*. Boston: Shambhala, 2004.

Patrul Rinpoche. *The Words of My Perfect Teacher*. Translated by the Padmakara Translation Group. Boston: Shambhala, 1998.

Ponlop, Dzogchen. "Introduction." In *The Thirty-Seven Practices of a Bodhisattva* by Ngulchu Tokmé. New York: Nitartha International, 1994.

Rinchen, Geshe Sonam. *The Thirty-Seven Practices of Bodhisattvas*. Translated by Ruth Sonam. Ithaca, NY: Snow Lion, 1997.

Shantideva. *The Way of the Bodhisattva*. Translated by the Padmakara Translation Group. Boston: Shambhala, 1997.

———. *A Guide to the Bodhisattva's Way of Life*. Translated by Stephen Batchelor. Dharamsala: Library of Tibetan Works and Archives, 1979.

Thondup, Tulku. *Masters of Meditation and Miracles: Lives of the Great Buddhist Masters of India and Tibet*. Boston: Shambhala, 1999.

Wangmo, Jamyang. *The Lawudo Lama: Stories of Reincarnation from the Mount Everest Region*. Boston: Wisdom, 2005.

Zahler, Leah. *Study and Practice of Meditation: Tibetan Interpretations of the Concentrations & Formless Absorptions*. Ithaca, NY: Snow Lion, 2009.

Index

ABOUT THE TRANSLATOR
Brief Notes on the Life of Christopher Stagg

Christopher Warren Stagg (1977–2018) was a gifted translator, teacher, Buddhist practitioner, singer, and musician. A close student of his spiritual teacher, Dzogchen Ponlop Rinpoche, Chris served as a Tibetan-to-English oral interpreter and literary translator of a wide range of Buddhist teachings, including his landmark translation of the *Hundred Thousand Songs of Milarepa* (Shambhala, 2017) and the present volume.

Born on September 3, 1977, in Starkville, Mississippi, Chris displayed considerable talent in relation to both language and music, particularly singing, from an early age. He and his family moved to Knoxville, Tennessee, during his high school years. Following his graduation from high school, he relocated to Westminster, Colorado. Having participated robustly in various choir and theater groups in his local areas, he graduated from the University of Colorado-Boulder with a bachelor of arts in vocal performance in 1999. Chris grew up within the Christian tradition and was raised as a Southern Baptist. Despite maintaining a lifelong appreciation for Christianity, it was during his time in Boulder that Chris developed a deep and abiding interest in Buddhism. During this period, he met Dzogchen Ponlop Rinpoche and formed a spiritual connection that would eventually blossom into a meaningful teacher-student relationship.

Chris spent a year in residence at Gampo Abbey Monastery in Nova Scotia, Canada, from 2001 to 2002. At Gampo Abbey, he engaged in intensive meditation, study, mindful work, and community building, and held the discipline of temporary monastic vows. He moved to Seattle to be with the Nalandabodhi sangha at its international seat, Nalanda West, in 2003. His early years in the Pacific Northwest saw him complete a master of arts in music education at the University of Washington in 2006. During this period, Chris taught music in public schools and progressed in his music career, highlighted by his time singing with the innovative and internationally praised choral group, The Esoterics. While continuing to diligently pursue his path of Buddhist study and meditation, Chris also emerged as a leader in his sangha, serving as codirector of Nalandabodhi Seattle from 2004 through 2006. Chris was also an active practice instructor in Nalandabodhi, mentoring students for many years along the paths of study, meditation, and mindful activity.

Chris began his study of the Tibetan language in the early 2000s. His interest in learning the language increased steadily, and a few years later he encountered opportunities for intensive studies of Tibetan language and Buddhist philosophy. He traveled for his studies to India and Nepal, first in 2007, and again from 2010 to 2013. Notable among the institutions at which Chris studied are the Vajra Vidya Institute in Varanasi, India, and Thrangu Tashi Yangtse Monastery in the Namo Buddha region of Nepal.

In the early 2010s, Chris began more actively serving his guru, Dzogchen Ponlop Rinpoche. He joined the staff of the Office of Dzogchen Ponlop Rinpoche in 2013 and was appointed deputy chief of staff in 2015. He also served as a personal secretary, attendant, and oral interpreter for Rinpoche, traveling with and assisting him in his teaching and touring activities throughout North America, Asia, and Europe. Naturally attentive and gracious, he helped countless students and hosting organizations by facilitating their communications with Rinpoche and tending to their needs.

Chris's skills as an oral interpreter began to accelerate during this period. In addition to serving as an oral interpreter for Dzogchen Ponlop Rinpoche on many occasions throughout the world, he translated for Dilyak Drupon Rinpoche at multiple Nalandabodhi Canada retreat programs. He served as an oral interpreter for various acharyas, especially Acharya Lama Tenpa Gyaltsen, at the Nitartha Institute Summer Program from 2013 through 2018.

Some of his noteworthy accomplishments in oral interpretation include: a month-long Nitartha Institute *Abhidharmakosha* intensive seminar taught by Acharya Kelzang Wangdi in May of 2016 and courses taught by Acharya Lama Tenpa Gyaltsen on Lama Mipham's *Beacon of Certainty* at the Nitartha Institute summer programs from 2014 through 2018. He served as an oral interpreter for acharyas and lamas throughout this same period at the annual Nalandabodhi Sangha Retreat and at other programs throughout North America.

In terms of written translations, in addition to the present volume and the magnum opus of Milarepa mentioned earlier, Chris produced written translations for each of the annual *Beacon of Certainty* courses mentioned above. He also translated most of Shamar Mipham Chökyi Wangchuk's *Smiling Radiance of the Laughing Manjughosha*, a text on valid cognition, for a Nitartha Institute program taught by Acharya Kelzang Wangdi in Warsaw, Poland. He translated a wealth of other texts and liturgies from both the common vehicles' traditions and the lineages of definitive meaning instructions.

Chris's formidable, famed, and highly refined singing and musical skills would also benefit practitioners of the Dharma directly. Following in a tradition initiated through the blessings of Khenpo Tsültrim Gyamtso Rinpoche, Chris translated many songs of realization of Milarepa and other great masters, setting them to contemporary melodies. He arranged several of his translations of meditation liturgies so they could be sung to traditional Tibetan or Sanskrit melodies. He was the main musical composer and arranger for His Holiness the Seventeenth Gyalwang Karmapa, Ogyen Trinley Dorjes's "Aspiration for the World." A musical arrangement he made for a translation of Dza Patrul Rinpoche's "The Five Poisons Self-Liberated" stands as a favorite "Dharma song" for many.

When touring in support of his translation of *The Hundred Thousand Songs of Milarepa*, Chris would often teach through the medium of song and melody. He engaged with and served the Nalandabodhi community in a wide variety of musical ways, including leading regular "Songs of Realization" group singing sessions at Nalanda West. To remember Chris is to instantly recall the power of his voice to transform and delight any gathering; he would often be called upon to sing a verse or song expressing key points of contemplative instruction.

Chris was widely and deeply loved by many, and news of his passing due to an automobile accident on October 1, 2018, was a grave shock and a difficult-to-receive teaching on the impermanent nature of the precious human body. Nevertheless, through this book and the other translations he produced, the songs he composed and shared, and the inspiration he provoked in many hearts, the marks of Chris's genuine warmth and pure intention will continue to appear, inform, and enlighten.

This biography relied in part on a tribute to Christopher Stagg written shortly after his passing by Juli Goetz Morser.